GREATEST GOALIES

OF THE

NHL

Stories of the Legendary Players

J. Alexander Poulton

OVER
TIME
BOOKS

The Publisher: OverTime Books is an imprint of Éditions de la
Montagne Verte

Library and Archives Canada Cataloguing in Publication

Poulton, J. Alexander (Jay Alexander), 1977–
    Greatest goalies of the NHL: stories of the legendary
    players/ J. Alexander Poulton.

Includes bibliographical references.
ISBN 10: 1-897277-12-1
ISBN 13: 978-1-897277-12-6

    1. Hockey goalkeepers—Biography. 2. National Hockey
League—Biography. I. Title.

GV848.5.A1P693 2006   796.962092'2   C2006-906168-8

Project Director: J. Alexander Poulton
Proofreader: Brian Crane
Cover Image: Courtesy of Getty Images Sport, photography by
Jim McIsaac

PC:P5

Acknowledgements

I would like to thank all the guys I played hockey with as a kid on those late nights under the street lamps on Bernier Street and the parents for putting up with us (except the grumpy couple who used to call the cops). I was always too small and didn't have the necessary aggression to play forward, so the other kids put me in goal, and I have played that position ever since. Growing up in Montréal, most kids who played in nets wanted to be Patrick Roy, but for some reason, I always chose Brian Hayward.

Contents

Chapter 4: PLAYOFF HEROES

Chapter 5: GOALTENDING FACT CHECK

Introduction

"You don't have to be crazy to be a goalie,
but it helps!"
—Bernie Parent

"Sixty minutes of Hell!"
—Glenn Hall

There is no other position in professional sports that measures up to the constant pressures, pains and pleasures of a hockey goaltender. It takes a special kind of person to put themselves in the path of frozen pucks traveling in excess of 100 kilometres per hour, but once they put on the pads for the first time, most never leave. Not many young players decide to be goaltenders—the position just finds them. Many professionals will tell the story of how they always wanted to be a goal-scoring forward, but because they could not skate well or their older brother wouldn't let them play up front, they got put in goal. For the ones who stayed in goal, they found a position unlike any other in professional sports. The constant pressure that falls on the goaltender's shoulders, the pain of having five players trying to put a frozen puck in the net and the fact that there are no other players on the team to relate these problems to make it necessary to have a specific personality type. Alone for the majority of the game (besides the occasional word from the defencemen), a goaltender must be at ease and be able to talk through problems without any help. On their own most of the time, many goaltenders develop into unique characters.

Terry Sawchuk, one of the greatest goaltenders of all time, dealt with the pain and pressure of his position by withdrawing into himself and expressing his emotions in angry outbursts. Many nights, he got into shouting matches with other players and even with fans. One can hardly blame him for his reactions after a lifetime of pulled muscles, bruises and over 400 stitches to his face.

Then there are goaltenders such as Patrick Roy, who competed with the same drive and ferocity as guys like Sawchuk but expressed themselves in different ways. Superstitious, Roy used to talk to his posts before, during and after games to make sure they were ready to help him out when he needed it. Or you can look at Jacques Plante, who constantly knitted toques and always had to put on his goaltending equipment in a specific order. No one ever complained too much about their eccentricities because the quirks seemed to make the goalies feel better, and if they felt better, they played better.

Stripped of all the extras, goaltending comes down to a mental game. Naturally, goaltenders have to work on strength, speed and skating, but the best weapon for any player between the posts is his mind. It is the common thread that is found in all of the great goaltenders. They are only human, and on many nights, even the best, including Patrick Roy and Terry Sawchuk, had bad games filled with soft goals. It was their ability to bounce back from a soft goal and make the saves that counted and made them Hall of Fame goaltenders.

No other goaltender better exemplified those qualities than Patrick Roy. He knew everything about the game. He devoured opposing player statistics, watched game footage of opponents and took down notes on where they would shoot. He possessed a unique vision of the ice surface, could read how a play would develop and be in position before the puck got near the net. During his greatest years, he made every save look easy because he put in hours and hours of work before each game. Even an old-school goaltender like Jacques Plante kept numerous notebooks on some of the best goal scorers in the league so that when he was face to face with one of them on a breakaway he would know what the player was most likely to try. The goalies would tell you the preparation didn't always work, but that just made the great goaltenders try even harder to make the save next time—and in goaltending, you can always be sure there will be a next time.

In the pages ahead, you will find some of the greatest goaltenders to ever put on a set of pads, from Paddy Moran to Martin Brodeur. The style of equipment has changed, and the players have gotten bigger and faster, but the job of a goaltender has and always will be to stop pucks.

Chapter One

THE EARLY DAYS (1893–1942)

Paddy Moran

Back when moustaches and top hats were in fashion and goalies were called goalkeepers, there were a few brave souls who donned their cricket pads and took up the position between the posts during some of the most violent days in hockey history.

With a name befitting his era, Paddy Moran began his big-league playing days in 1905 in his hometown of Québec City with the Québec Bulldogs franchise of the Eastern Canada Amateur Hockey Association. After posting good numbers with his minor league teams, Moran moved into position between the pipes for the Bulldogs with a lot of potential. However, a goaltender can have all the talent in the world, but with a terrible team in front of him, it is difficult for him to post a winning record and a decent goals-against average. That was exactly the problem Moran faced in his first years with the Québec Bulldogs.

In the 10 games that he played for the Bull-dogs during the 1905–06 season, Moran posted a dismal record of three wins and seven losses with a goals-against average of 6.79. The modern hockey fan would look at those stats and come to the conclusion that Moran was simply a bad goaltender. But with an incompetent team before him, Moran's record was not as bad as it could have been.

Whether his teammates were floundering about on the ice or sitting in the penalty box, Moran was consistently the best player on a bad team, which made his talents in goal all the more impressive. Numbers are always important, but they never tell the whole story. Moran's perseverance during the lean years made him stand out as one of the best goaltenders of his time.

Lester Patrick, who knew a thing or two about goaltending himself, once commented on Moran's skill in between the pipes: "I would pick Paddy Moran of Québec and Percy LeSueur of Ottawa for goal. In their heyday, Moran and LeSueur were two of the smartest goalers I ever saw in action."

Being a smart goaltender in those days often meant making your presence on the ice well known to the opposing players so they would not get too adventurous near the net, and

Moran was the ultimate intimidator. For those who think that the early days of hockey were a time when gentlemen played the sport and conducted themselves on the ice according to the rules of the game, think again. They might have been gentlemen off the ice, but once the skates were on and the puck was dropped, all the social niceties were gone. No goaltender was more renowned for his short temper in hockey's early days than Paddy Moran.

The number one priority for a goaltender is to keep the puck out of the net, and to do that, he has to see the puck. Moran made sure he had a clear view of the puck by swinging his stick like a lumberjack swings an axe, clear-cutting the opposing players out from in front of his net. This was especially true early on in his career with the Québec Bulldogs, when more often than not, the opposing players would be at his end of the rink most of the game. Moran was without a doubt the best member of the Bulldogs team on the ice, but his ill-tempered ways often got him in trouble with the referees.

The now-defunct *Montréal Star* newspaper described Moran's actions after a 1910 game between the Bulldogs and the Montréal Canadiens. "Paddy Moran was very strong in his work last night, but also very short-tempered. It was due to the referees both being busy watching the play at the Canadiens' end of the rink that he did not get a serious penalty meted out to him when he tried to slash Henri Dallaire's head off with one lightning stroke of his hockey blade."

Moran had many more tricks up his sleeves to keep the puck out of the goal and opposing players away from his net. During his playing days, there was no painted area that designated the crease, so it was Moran's job to teach the other players what line not to cross. When they crossed that line, the rules no longer applied in Moran's view of the game. Never without his healthy wad of chewing tobacco stuffed in his cheek, one of Moran's favorite ways of letting someone know that he had crossed into his territory was to spit a stream of tobacco juice into the face of the player bearing down on the net. But Moran did not have to use his guerilla tactics for much longer. In 1911, the Québec Bulldogs finally iced a competitive team, and Moran could focus on playing his position to perfection.

With quality players like Joe Malone, Joe Hall and Jack Macdonald on the team scoring at regular intervals, the Bulldogs went from the bottom of the league straight to the top. Going from just three wins in the previous season, Moran improved his record to 10–8, giving his team a chance to play for the Stanley Cup in a two-game series against the Moncton Victorias.

The Bulldogs convincingly won the first game by a score of 9–3, and Moran shut out the Victorias in the second game 8–0 to win the Bulldogs' first ever Stanley Cup. Moran repeated his stellar performance next season, backstopping the Bulldogs to a 16–4 record in the 1912–13 season. He was once again the deciding factor as the team took home their second consecutive Stanley Cup title by defeating the Maritime champion Sydney Millionaires in a two-game series by a combined score of 20–5.

Although the Bulldogs never won the Stanley Cup again, Moran kept the team competitive over the next few years until the National Hockey Association folded in 1917. The Québec Bulldogs decided not to join the new National Hockey League. Not wanting to play in any other city, Moran chose to hang up his pads and retire from the game he loved.

Fellow netminder Percy LeSueur once wrote of Moran in his *Handbook of Hockey*, "He was the most spectacular goalkeeper I have ever seen."

For his teammates, he was sadly missed. For his opponents, they were really happy when he retired.

Percy LeSueur

In the early days of hockey, goaltenders had the toughest job on the ice. With thin cricket pads on their legs and a slightly enlarged stick, goaltenders looked nothing like the armor-plated netminders of today. Percy LeSueur played in nets during the era of the goal scorer, when players like Joe Malone and Tommy Smith scored over 25 goals each in a 16-game season. Scoring during regular games was high, and so was the goals-against average of most goaltenders, but LeSueur was not like any other goaltender. He played with excellent athleticism and was as quick with his hands and feet as he was in reading how a play would develop.

But like many early players, LeSueur did not start out as a goaltender. While playing in his hometown of Québec City, LeSueur played as a right-winger for several amateur teams and was known for his great speed and offensive touch on the attack. But fate had a different plan for LeSueur. When he transferred to Smith Falls, Ontario, to play for their Senior League team, he was put in between the pipes for the first time when the regular goaltender could not make a game due to illness. The team's management was so impressed with how LeSueur played that they decided to keep him in nets. He struggled a bit in his first full season as goaltender, winning three games and losing three, but his goals-against average was an incredible 2.11. Other goaltenders of his era, such as Harry 'Hap' Holmes, recorded averages as high as 7.33 and 6.00.

In LeSueur's second season between the pipes for Smith Falls, the hockey world began to take notice. After an incredible regular season in the Senior Ontario Hockey League, winning all seven of the games when he tended goal, Smith Falls decided to send a formal challenge to the defending Stanley Cup champion Ottawa Senators to play in a two-game total-goals series for the Stanley Cup. The Ottawa Senators were into their fourth year as Stanley Cup champions and were not about to let a small team from Smith Falls take the Cup away from them, but Smith Falls felt confident in their challenge as long as they had a healthy Percy LeSueur in nets.

No one expected Smith Falls to win against the mighty Senators, but LeSueur kept his team in the game with some of the most spectacular goaltending of his time. The *Montréal Star* newspaper reported the events the next day. "The most spectacular saves of the match were made by LeSueur. Three of Ottawa's forwards got right down on him when there was no defenceman near enough to help him. First Frank McGee, then Rat Westwick, then Harry Smith shot, but on each occasion, though they were only a yard or two away, he managed to stop the puck and get it to safety. The way he stopped the most dangerous shots was a sight rarely seen."

Despite the inspired performance, the Senators still managed to slip 6 goals by LeSueur to win the game 6–5. In the second game, the Senators completely dominated the game, winning by a final score of 8–2 and retaining their title as Stanley Cup champions. But LeSueur was the story of the series. The Ottawa Senators were so impressed that just one week later they offered him a contract to play with them after they were defeated in another Stanley Cup challenge by the Montréal Wanderers 9–1. LeSueur's impact with his new team was felt immediately. Although the Wanderers jumped to an early 1–0 lead, LeSueur did not disappoint his new teammates and played with the same athleticism and skill that he had displayed against the Senators just one week earlier. With the confidence that their new goaltender could keep them in the game, the Senators mounted an incredible comeback, scoring 9 unanswered goals to tie the total-goals series at 9 goals each. Luckily for the Wanderers, their team leader, Lester Patrick, scored two late-period goals on LeSueur to wrestle the

Stanley Cup out of the hands of a disappointed but proud Ottawa Senators team. One positive thing they took away from the loss was that they now had a goaltender who could lead them back to the ultimate goal of all hockey players—the Stanley Cup.

Since goaltenders were prohibited from falling to the ice to stop the puck, LeSueur developed an attacking, wandering style that kept him in the action instead of sitting back in his net. On more than one occasion, LeSueur would dart out of his net when a player came in on a break-away and try to poke the puck away, or more often, simply deliver a devastating check before the opponent could shoot.

Ever the student of the game, LeSueur was always looking for ways to improve his play. Prior to LeSueur, most goaltenders used the same gloves as the players, but realizing that goal-tenders had a different job to perform, LeSueur developed a pad for the goaltender's gauntlet that protected his hands from the incoming shots. In 1911, he patented the LeSueur net, which was used in professional hockey from 1912–25 until the net with the current dimensions was adopted as the standard. But his contributions to the game didn't end on the ice. In 1909, he wrote a 48-page booklet titled *How to Play Hockey*, which gave instructions on how to play the game with some basic strategies to employ against opponents.

In his eight seasons with the Ottawa Senators, LeSueur won the Cup two times and became one of the premiere goaltenders in all the hockey leagues. LeSueur was so well respected by his teammates and the owners that he even captained, coached and managed the team for a period. One of the proudest moments in his career came in 1908, when he was selected in the first ever all-star game in hockey history that was played to benefit the family of Montréal Wanderers forward Hod Stuart, who had died in a construction accident.

By 1914 the Ottawa Senators were no longer the dominant team they once were, so LeSueur was sent off to the Toronto Shamrocks for the start of the 1914–15 National Hockey Association season. Things did not go well for the now-veteran goaltender in his new Toronto home, and by the end of the following season he retired from the game in favour of combat duty during World War I with Canada's 48th Highlanders regiment.

After returning from the war, he could not stay away from the game he loved, and he made his living as a referee, coach, arena operator and journalist. LeSueur worked as a newspaper columnist and was an original member of *Hockey Night in Canada*'s "Hot Stove," in which journalists and players discussed hockey during intermission.

Percy LeSueur was eventually inducted into the Hockey Hall of Fame in 1961. Just a year later he died at the age of 81 on January 27, 1962.

Georges Vézina

Most people know his name because of the trophy that rewards the best goaltender in the National Hockey League each year, but few know about the life of the man himself. The simple, calm and collected man from Chicoutimi, Québec, had a life marred by tragedy off the ice. Of the 24 (yes, 24) children his wife gave birth to, only two made it into adulthood. For Vézina, hockey became a way of dealing with his personal tragedies and bringing some joy into his life.

Hockey was in its first few years of exis-tence when Vézina joined the hockey team in his hometown. Right from the start, Vézina knew he wanted to be a goaltender. He had the calm demeanor and nerves of steel that were necessary for someone who would face down frozen pucks all game. Like many goaltenders at the time, Vézina played hockey in his boots and did not learn how to skate until he was 18 years old. But his ability on the ice kept getting better and better with age, and soon bigger clubs began to take notice.

Playing for the local Chicoutimi club, Vézina was first noticed when he shut out the visiting Grand-Mère Senior Club, who was touring the countryside to prepare for their Allan Cup appearance. The Grand-Mère players were confident that they could defeat the backwater Chicoutimi team, but they had not counted on Georges Vézina tending goal.

After he shut the Grand-Mère Club down twice, it was time for the visiting Montréal Canadiens to get a taste of what Vézina could do in goal. Keep in mind that shutouts in hockey were not a common thing at the time. In his entire professional career, Percy LeSueur recorded only five shutouts, and Paddy Moran only had two in 18 years. When the Canadiens visited with their team of high-powered professionals, they were surprised that Vézina erected a brick wall in front of the Chicoutimi net and shut them out.

In Kevin Allen and Bob Duff's book, *Without Fear,* A.J. Vézina, the great-grand nephew of Georges Vézina said, "There were at least three games in Chicoutimi between the Canadiens and the Chicoutimi team, and each time, Chicoutimi won, thanks to Georges' goaltending."

Canadiens netminder Joseph Cattarinch was so impressed with Vézina's abilities in goal that he urged Canadiens management to sign him even though it meant that he would lose his position on the team. Vézina first put on his jersey for the start of the 1910–11 National Hockey Association (NHA) season.

Competition was pretty fierce among the goaltenders that season. The Québec Bulldogs' Paddy Moran, Ottawa's Percy LeSueur and the Montréal Wanderer's Riley Hern all were vying for the top spot. Vézina finished at the top of the league with a goals-against average of 3.80.

The following season the Canadiens struggled, but Vézina kept up his spectacular displays on the ice and again took home the best goaltender in the league with the lowest goals-against average. Vézina was so calm and relaxed in nets that he quickly earned himself the nickname the "Chicoutimi Cucumber" because he was as cool as a cucumber in front of any opponents.

Although the Canadiens faltered during Vézina's first few years, they finally turned things around for the 1913–14 NHA season. Vézina recorded a goals-against average of 3.14 and led the league with 13 wins and 7 losses. The Toronto Blueshirts took home the Cup that year, but the Canadiens now had the quality players in front of Vézina to have a shot at winning the franchise's first-ever Stanley Cup. Just two years later, the Canadiens finally found themselves in a position to become Stanley Cup champions.

Led offensively by Newsy Lalonde and Didier Pitre, the Canadiens finished the regular season at the top of the NHA standings with sixteen wins, seven losses and one tie. Vézina had another outstanding season in nets with a 3.08 goals-against average, only bested by league rival Ottawa Senators goaltender Clint Benedict. Winning the NHA championship, the Canadiens earned the right to face off against the Pacific Coast Hockey League champions, the Portland Rosebuds, for the Stanley Cup.

Vézina was instrumental in the Canadiens push for their first-ever Stanley Cup, using his quick reflexes and ability to read how a play would develop in order to keep his team in the final series. It was close, but the Canadiens managed to take the series 3–2 thanks to Vézina's stingy 2.60 goals-against average.

Most players have their best years when they first start out in the league, and they tend to produce less and less as time goes on. But with Vézina, as time passed he just got better and better. After a disappointing 1919 push for the Stanley Cup that was cancelled because of the influenza virus that killed teammate Joe Hall, the Canadiens were forced to rebuild their team, making Vézina's job a little more difficult in goal.

By the 1922–23 season, things began to turn around for the Canadiens as they improved their winning ways. Vézina had his best season so far with a goals-against average of 2.46. The next season, the Canadiens came back with a more youthful-looking lineup, with future Hall of Fame members such as Howie Morenz, Aurele Joliat and Billy Boucher. While they needed this new influx of young talent to secure the goals that would win them another Stanley Cup, Vézina held the fort until the new players arrived and kept the team respectable during the rebuilding years.

The 1923–24 season opened poorly for the Canadiens. In their first 12 games, they went a measly 4–8 despite Vézina's reliable goaltending. But the Canadiens turned it completely around for the last half of the season and finished strongly with a record of 13–11. More importantly, Vézina finished with a 1.97 goals-against average. They

had a spot in the NHL finals against the Ottawa
Senators.

Vézina was stellar in the first game, turning
away everything the Senators shot as the Canadiens took the game by securing their slim 1–0
lead. Ottawa was simply outpaced in the first
game by Howie Morenz and Aurele Joliat and
Vézina's goaltending. The Canadiens won the second game 4–2 to move on to the Stanley Cup
finals against the Western League champs, the
Vancouver Millionares of the Pacific Coast Hockey
Association (PCHA) and the Calgary Tigers of the
Western Canadian Hockey League (WCHL).

In the first series of the two-tiered Stanley
Cup finals against Vancouver, Vézina held the
fort in a close series and came out the victor with
a score of 3–2 in game one and 2–1 in game two.
Calgary had an even more difficult time getting
pucks by Vézina, who only let in one goal in the
first game and had a shutout in the second, winning the series and his second Stanley Cup.

In Douglas Hunter's book, *A Breed Apart*,
Vancouver forward Frank Boucher, who faced
Vézina's tough goaltending during the finals on
many occasions, looked back years later on that
series and the man the Canadiens relied on to
stop the pucks. "The first thing that pops into my
mind is that he always wore a toque, a small,

knitted hat with no brim in Montréal colours—
bleu, blanc et rouge [blue, white and red]. I also
remember him as the coolest man I ever saw,
absolutely imperturbable. He stood upright
in the net and scarcely left his feet; he simply
played all his shots in a standing position. Vézina
was a pale, narrow-featured fellow, almost frail
looking, yet remarkably good with his stick. He'd
pick off more shots with it than he did with his
glove."

Vézina played his best season with the
Canadiens in 1924–25 with a 1.81 goals-against
average and another berth in the NHL playoffs.
Vézina recorded an amazing performance in the
NHL semifinals against the Toronto St. Patricks
but couldn't keep everything out of the net in the
Stanley Cup finals against the Victoria Cougars
of the Western Canada Hockey League (WCHL).
They went on to defeat the Canadiens three games
to one to win the Stanley Cup. (This was the last
time a Western League team won the Stanley
Cup. Just two years later, the Cup became the sole
property of the National Hockey League.)

Vézina left Montréal and immediately returned
to his family home in Chicoutimi. He had never
gotten used to living in the big city, preferring to
be out in nature rather than on the city streets.
But when he returned to camp for the start of
the 1925–26 season, it seemed his time in the

country did him more harm than good. His teammates were the first to notice that he was looking rather gaunt and frail from all the weight he had lost, and several times in practices, he had to sit on the bench for a while because he was so fatigued. Not one to complain, Vézina brushed off suggestions that he go see a doctor and suited up for Montréal's first game on November 25, 1925 against the Pittsburgh Pirates.

Vézina managed to play through a scoreless first intermission, but he looked like he was struggling just to stay on his feet on every save he made. The moment he got in the Canadiens' dressing room during the intermission, he spat up some blood and passed out. After regaining consciousness, Vézina refused to listen to the advice of the team doctor and his teammates. They wanted replacement goaltender Alphonse "Frenchy" Lacroix to take over in nets, even though Vézina had played 367 consecutive games. Despite his 39° temperature, Vézina proudly reassumed his place in goal, but before the referee could drop the puck, Vézina fell to the ice with blood dripping from the corner of his mouth. He was carried off the ice on a stretcher, and Lacroix took over in net for the remainder of the game.

Doctors informed Vézina that he had tuberculosis and that he did not have much longer to live. Near the end of the season, Vézina returned from Chicoutimi to Montréal one last time to break the news to Canadiens general manager Leo Dandurand and no one else. Seeing Vézina back in the building, the Canadiens' trainer in charge of equipment laid out Vézina's gear, thinking that he would be playing that night. Vézina did not tell him otherwise because he figured the team would play better if they thought he was coming back.

"It was his last act of devotion to the club," said Dandurand, looking back on that day.

Vézina visited the Canadiens dressing room one last time, sat in his regular spot, and shed a few tears for the team and the game he loved. He took home his 1924 Stanley Cup–winning jersey as a souvenir.

On March 24, 1926, after months of agonizing pain, Vézina finally succumbed to the disease. The following year, the Canadiens donated the Vézina Memorial Trophy honouring the best goaltender during the NHL's regular season. To this day, when people think of the best in goaltending, Vézina's name always comes up.

Harry "Hap" Holmes

Not many people know the name Harry "Hap" Holmes, but his list of achievements ranks with some of the greatest goaltenders of his time. A journeyman goaltender, he was never part of one team for long, but with every team he played for, he always made a significant impact. From 1912 to 1928, he played in all the top professional leagues in Canada—the National Hockey Association (NHA), the Pacific Coast Hockey Association (PCHA), the Western Canada Hockey League (WCHL), the Western Hockey League (WHL), and the National Hockey League (NHL)—and backstopped four of those teams all the way to the Stanley Cup championship.

Holmes' winning touch began as soon as he turned pro with the Toronto Blueshirts of the NHA, helping the team establish themselves in a league dominated for the past two years by goaltender Paddy Moran and his Québec Bulldog squad. In his sophomore year with Toronto, Holmes had an excellent season, putting the Blueshirts in contention for the Stanley Cup against Georges Vézina's Montréal Canadiens. Holmes was the better player this time around as Toronto took the series on the strength of their goaltender's performance by a score of 6–2 in the two-game total-goal series.

During that series with the Canadiens, many criticized Holmes because of his apparent indifference in stopping the puck. Although Holmes was obviously good at stopping pucks on a consistent basis, he had a lack of flair for the dramatic that had some worried that he was a lazy goaltender. His calm demeanor belied the fact that Holmes was an outstanding tactician and a great technical goaltender who knew how to play the angles.

After just three seasons with the Toronto Blueshirts, Holmes joined up with the Seattle Metropolitans of the PCHA. His sophomore luck continued with Seattle as he backstopped his team to the first Stanley Cup won outside of the Dominion of Canada. Either Holmes had a knack for being in the right place at the right time, or he was truly a clutch goaltender that a playoff contender could rely on. The year after his Cup win with the Metropolitans, Holmes was loaned out to the Toronto Arenas of the fledgling National Hockey League, and he promptly won another Stanley Cup in 1918. After beating Georges Vézina and the Montréal Canadiens in the NHL finals in a closely contested total-goals series, Toronto hosted challengers the Vancouver Millionaires in a five-game series to decide the championship. Holmes led the way in a hard-fought series that went the full five games. Toronto came out the victors in the final game by a score of 2–1, thanks to their goaltender, Holmes.

In his book *Without Fear*, Kevin Allen cites an article written in the *Toronto Globe* about Holmes' performance during the final game of the series. "Holmes was at the top of his form and made stops in all three periods that were a little short of marvelous. From all angles, the net guardian swept the puck in the corner, kicking away the low ones, jumping into the waist-high shots, and cuffing with hand and glove those shots that were driven at him shoulder high."

But once again, Holmes was on the move, back to Seattle for the 1918–19 campaign that brought him back into the Stanley Cup finals against the Montréal Canadiens. The series was a classic battle between eastern and western clubs, but it was unfortunately stopped because of the outbreak of Spanish influenza that put several players in the hospital. Holmes had another shot in the playoffs just one year later with the Seattle Metropolitans against the mighty Ottawa Senators. He did his best to keep his team in the series, taking them all the way to the fifth and deciding game. But the Senators' high-powered forwards, Frank Nighbor and Jack Darragh, were too much for Holmes and he let in six goals in the final game to lose another chance at the Cup.

After several more unsuccessful years, the Seattle Metropolitans folded, and Holmes moved once again, this time to the Victoria Cougars of the WCHL. Victoria cruised to a 3–1 series victory to become the last non-NHL team to win the Stanley Cup.

Holmes had won his fourth Stanley Cup with his fourth different team. He returned the following year to defend his title against the NHL champion Montréal Maroons, but he could not stop Nels Stewart from putting in six goals in the series. The Victoria forwards could get nothing by Maroon goaltender Clint Benedict, who recorded three shutouts in each of his team's victories. After the Cougars' defeat, the WCHL folded because of financial difficulties. Holmes again found himself on the move, this time to the Detroit Cougars of the NHL.

Holmes continued to produce great numbers, recording 11 shutouts and a 1.73 goals-against average in the 1927–28 regular season, but he didn't have the same desire to play the game he once had and announced his retirement after that season. Harry Holmes died 12 years later while vacationing in Florida. Immediately after, a trophy was inaugurated in his name to honour the top goalie in the American Hockey League. He was inducted into the Hockey Hall of Fame in 1972.

Clint Benedict

At a time when hockey was constantly changing, Clint Benedict was the game's most innovative and creative player when it came to his position. In an era where most goaltenders were small and light, Benedict was the first big goaltender at 6' tall and close to 200 pounds. But his size wasn't the only new thing that Benedict brought to hockey.

Upon entering the professional ranks with the Ottawa Senators for the 1912–13 National Hockey Association regular season, Benedict took aim at a rule that he thought was simply ridiculous given the nature of his position. Long established in the rules of the National Hockey Association, goaltenders were not allowed to make a save by falling to the ice. If they did so intentionally, they would received a minor penalty for the infraction. Never one to conform to regulations, Benedict set out on a lengthy campaign to get the rules changed in his favour.

Benedict developed a unique acting ability on the ice—whenever he wanted to make a save along the ice, he would fake loosing his balance and fall to the ice. For years, Benedict put referees on the spot constantly until they began bringing their grievances to higher powers.

Critics and the media gave Benedict a healthy supply of nicknames for his flaunting of the rules, such as "Praying Benny' and "Tumbling Clint," since he spent so much time sprawled out on the ice.

For five years, Benedict continued his acting routine on the ice until the league had had enough. During the new National Hockey League's inaugural 1917–18 season, referees took their complaints to league president Frank Calder, who finally changed the rule on January 9, 1918, allowing goaltenders to fall to the ice. Calder spoke of the rule change in an interview with the *Montréal Star* newspaper. "In the future, they can fall on their knees, or stand on their heads, if they think they can stop the puck better in that way than by standing on their feet," said Calder. Benedict got his wish and no longer needed an Oscar-winning performance to stop a puck. He used his newfound freedom to lead the Ottawa Senators back to their former glory and their position at the top of the league.

Benedict began a five-year run as the league's top goaltender with the lowest goals-against average. His Ottawa Senators also found themselves back in their place as the dominant team in the league. During the 1919–20 regular season, Benedict was the only goaltender in the league to register a shutout, and he had five in total that season—a major accomplishment during a time when shutouts were rare. For example, during the 1917–18 inaugural NHL season, there were only two recorded shutouts (Benedict and Vézina), and the following season, there were only three (Benedict two, Vézina one).

The 1919–20 season ended with the Senators winning both halves of the regular-season split schedule, giving them an automatic berth in the Stanley Cup finals against the PCHA champion Seattle Metropolitans.

The series was a hard-fought battle between two high-powered offensive teams, but Benedict managed to keep the scores low and out-duel Seattle goaltender Harry "Hap" Holmes to win his first-ever Stanley Cup championship. Over the next three years, Benedict backstopped the Senators to two more Stanley Cups and secured his place as one of the greatest goaltenders in hockey history.

But things were not over for the star goaltender. When the NHL expanded for the 1924–25 season with the addition of the Boston Bruins and the Montréal Maroons, Benedict was sent to the Maroons along with teammate Harry "Punch" Broadbent to help the Montréal team compete in the new market. After a shaky first season in the league, Benedict and the Montréal Maroons turned things around the next year, finishing just behind Benedict's former teammates, the Ottawa Senators. The Senators were still the best team in the league and were made even better by the outstanding goaltending of their young star, Alex Connell. In the NHL finals, Benedict faced off against his former teammates in a close two-game total-goal series. Benedict's veteran experience helped the Maroons defeat the Senators and the young Connell by a slim margin of 2–1, allowing the Maroons to move on to the Stanley Cup finals against the Victoria Cougars. Benedict recorded three shutouts against the overwhelmed Cougars squad and won his fourth career Stanley Cup.

He continued to play well for the Maroons for several more seasons. But one night, on January 7, 1930, during a game against the Montréal Canadiens, everything changed. Benedict's career took a turn for the worse when Canadiens legend Howie Morenz came speeding over the

Maroons blue line on one of his patented rushes and unleashed a blistering slap shot that caught Benedict in the cheekbone and nose. Benedict fell immediately to the ice and only woke up later when he was in the hospital. He had a fractured cheekbone and a broken nose and would be out of the Maroons lineup for at least a month.

He wanted back in the lineup right away, but his nose and cheek were still fragile, so Benedict had a crude leather facemask made to protect him from another shot. It was the first time in professional hockey history that a goaltender wore a facemask, almost 30 years before Jacques Plante first donned his mask. But Benedict quickly gave up on the idea after a 2–1 defeat in a game against Chicago that he blamed on the mask. It blocked his vision on low shots. He tried another mask like that of a catcher in baseball, but again, it proved to be a distraction. To make matters worse, during another game against the Canadiens, Howie Morenz unleashed a powerful shot that hit Benedict in the throat, putting him out of competition again. When he was ready to return to his regular duties in the Maroons net, he found out that he had been sent down to their minor league club, the Windsor Bulldogs. Benedict won the championship with the Bulldogs and retired from hockey after 17 years as a professional.

From hockey superstardom to relative obscurity, Benedict coached a British hockey team for several years, followed by a coaching job in Sherbrooke, Québec. He finally left hockey for good when he took a job with the City of Ottawa. The goaltender who revolutionized the game and was the best at his position for many years was passed over for induction into the Hockey Hall of Fame until they finally recognized his contributions to the game in 1965. He died 10 years later in an Ottawa hospital at the age of 84.

Alex Connell

If you needed a game-saving player able to turn the tide by simply being on the ice, you had to look no further than Alex Connell. With the lowest career goals-against average in National Hockey League history at 1.91, it is no wonder he is still considered one of the greatest clutch goaltenders of all time.

He began his career in 1924 with the Ottawa Senators, replacing goaltender Clint Benedict. After a shaky first season, Connell rebounded with his best career season with a record of 24 wins, 8 losses, and 4 ties. He had a career-low

1.12 goals-against average and led the league in shutouts with 15, but it wasn't enough to get the Senators into the Stanley Cup finals. The Montréal Maroons and Clint Benedict defeated them by just one goal.

The 1926–27 season saw the Senators at the top of the league once again thanks to Connell's goaltending. This time finishing with a record of 30 wins, 10 losses, and 4 ties, the Senators were in a good position to challenge for the Cup. They faced off against the Montréal Canadiens in the semifinals and Connell was outstanding, playing the angles like a veteran and deflecting shots without fear, only letting in one goal during the two-game total-goal series.

In the Stanley Cup final, Connell would not be beaten easily as he out-played Boston Bruins goaltender Hal Winkler in a tight physical series, never letting in more than one goal in a game. The Ottawa Senators defeated the Bruins in four games to win the Stanley Cup. Connell recorded the lowest ever goals-against average in NHL play-off history at 0.60 (a mark he shares with only one other goaltender, Tiny Thompson of the 1929 Cup-winning Boston Bruins).

Connell continued to play for the Senators through some good and bad years until they suspended operations for the 1931–32 season because of financial difficulties caused by the Depression. After playing one season in Detroit, Connell returned to his position in the Ottawa nets. However, just 15 games into the season, the Senators were at the bottom of the league, and there were whispers of discontent among many of the players blaming the goaltender for their misfortunes. Connell wasn't happy with the way the team was playing and felt he wasn't to blame because the team in front of him simply was not scoring enough goals. Things finally fell apart between Connell and the Senators in a game against the Rangers halfway through the season.

Connell let in 4 goals by the second period, and Ottawa coach Cy Denneny pulled the goalie out of the game in favour of Bill Beveridge. Passing Beveridge on the ice, Connell politely wished his replacement good luck and skated off the ice. In a move that another goaltender Patrick Roy would repeat in 1995, Connell went immediately over to the Ottawa coach after being pulled from the game. "Your move was the height of stupidity," Connell said, according to the *Toronto Globe*. Connell never played another game in a Senators jersey after that incident.

After sitting out most of the 1933–34 season, playing in only one game with the New York Americans, Connell finally found a home with the Montréal Maroons for the start of the 1934–35 campaign. After he had been gone from the game for nearly two seasons, few gave the former star much of a chance at succeeding in his new home. Connell would prove all his doubters wrong.

Connell had kept in shape during his time off, performing his duties as a fireman for the City of Ottawa. He was more than ready to face any challenge in his new season with the Maroons. Connell proved to be the perfect fit for the squad that built its team with a defensive system in mind. The Maroons were not the highest scoring team in the league, but they kept the goals against to a minimum and managed to work their way into second place in the Canadian Division.

No one gave the Maroons much of a chance in the playoffs as they started off against the powerful Chicago Blackhawks. Sports writers predicted that the series was going to be a defensive affair because both teams' goaltenders allowed the fewest goals during the regular season. Chicago goaltender Lorne Chabot and the Maroons' Alex Connell each had a shutout in the first game of the total-goal series, and they had to wait until overtime of the second game to decide who would move on to the next round. The Maroons turned out the victors in the series and went on to defeat the New York Rangers in the semi-finals and face off against the Toronto Maple Leafs for the Stanley Cup. Connell out-dueled Toronto goaltender Georges Hainsworth as the Maroons surprised everyone and swept the series in three games.

Toronto coach Tommy Gorman commented to the media after the final game, which ended with a score of 3–1 and Toronto out-shooting the Maroons 44–18. "I remember Connell as putting on the greatest goalkeeping performance in the history of hockey."

Connell played one more season with the Maroons before finally hanging up his pads for good in 1937. He was inducted into the Hockey Hall of Fame in 1958.

Georges Hainsworth

After he played 11 seasons in the minors and three years with the Western Saskatoon Cresents, the National Hockey League finally noticed the top-notch goaltending of Georges Hainsworth in 1926 when he was signed to the Montréal Canadiens. He had some large pads to fill, replacing Canadiens legend Georges Vézina only a year after he passed away, but Hainsworth was more than up to the task.

Acting on the advice of former Canadiens player Newsy Lalonde and in desperate need of a goaltender, Leo Dandurand signed Hainsworth on August 23, 1926. Lalonde was familiar with Hainsworth's work from his time spent out in the western leagues and knew that the diminutive but skilled goaltender would fit perfectly into the Canadiens system. In just his first season with the Canadiens, Hainsworth showed management and the fans that they made the right decision in bringing him to the NHL.

In his first three years with the Canadiens, he won the newly created Vezina Trophy, given to the goaltender that had allowed the fewest goals against during the NHL regular season. Hainsworth had a career season in 1928–29, when in 44 regular season games he allowed only 43 goals and registered 22 shutouts for the lowest goals-against average in NHL history, 0.92.

Although he posted such incredible numbers, some would have preferred Hainsworth to be a little more charismatic in nets like other goaltenders around the league who constantly bounced, dove and shouted all over the arena. The quiet and serene Hainsworth once sarcastically apologized for his lack of enthusiasm on the ice. "I'm sorry

I can't put on a show like some of the other goal-tenders. I can't look excited because I'm not," said Hainsworth. " I can't shout at other players because that's not my style. I can't dive on easy shots and make them look hard. I guess all I can do is stop pucks."

After Hainsworth's record-breaking season in 1928–29, the National Hockey League changed the rules to allow forward passing in an effort to increase goal scoring and make the game more exciting for the fans. Although Hainsworth would never again achieve his incredible statistics from the 1928–29 season, his goaltending skills did not falter.

After a mediocre 1929–30 campaign, the Canadiens made it into the playoffs to face the Chicago Blackhawks in the first round. Hainsworth was outstanding in the two-game total-goal series. The Canadiens defeated the Blackhawks by a score of 3–2. He only allowed one New York Rangers goal in the semifinals and brought the Canadiens back to the Stanley Cup finals for the first time since they lost to the Victoria Cougars in 1925. Although Boston was the heavy favorite, losing just five times during the regular season, the Canadiens were confident in front of Hainsworth's goaltending, and they defeated the defending champions in a two-game sweep of the best-of-three series.

After repeating as Stanley Cup champions in 1931, the Canadiens fell on hard times like most teams did during the Depression era. Following two years of early exits from the playoffs, the Canadiens traded Hainsworth to the Toronto Maple Leafs in return for Lorne Chabot. After three seasons with the Maple Leafs, taking the team into the playoffs each year but never winning the Stanley Cup, Hainsworth decided it was time to retire from hockey after 25 years in between the pipes.

Hainsworth was inducted into the Hockey Hall of Fame posthumously in 1961, 11 years after he tragically lost his life in a car accident.

Lorne Chabot

Great goaltenders post outstanding regular season numbers and can put their teams in a good position for the playoffs. Truly legendary goaltenders are made in the playoffs.

At 6'1" and 190 pounds, Lorne Chabot was remarkably quick for his size, a feature noticed by the scouts of a new franchise that was set to start operations for the 1926–27 season. Chabot broke into the National Hockey league with the New York Rangers in 1926 and found immediate success in the franchise's first year in the league as they finished in first place in the American Division. Unfortunately for the rookie goaltender, the Rangers lost their first-ever playoff series against the Boston Bruins. But just one year later, Chabot had his revenge.

Chabot and the Rangers dispensed of the lowly Pittsburgh Pirates in the opening round of the playoffs and met up with the Bruins in the semifinals to exact revenge for the Rangers' early exit the year before. While the regular season showed that the Bruins were statistically the better team, Chabot was the better goaltender, allowing only two goals in the series. The Rangers moved into the Stanley Cup finals for the first time after just years of existence. If Chabot thought it was easy getting past Pittsburgh and Boston, the Montréal Maroons had something completely different in mind for the New York goaltender.

The Maroons came out flying in the first game and did not relent in their attack on the Rangers net all game until they had put two pucks past Chabot while Clint Benedict shut out the Rangers. In the second game, things took a turn for the worse for the Rangers sophomore goaltender. In the second period of the game, Chabot was the unlucky recipient of a powerful Nels Stewart slapshot that struck him directly in the eye and forced him off the ice. In a now-legendary decision, Rangers coach Lester Patrick decided to replace Chabot in goal for the remainder of that game two. The Rangers miraculously ended up winning by a score of 2–1 in overtime. Patrick called up goaltender Joe Miller to play out the rest of the series as the Rangers went on to win their first-ever Stanley Cup. Chabot could only sit on the sidelines and watch as his team played excellent hockey without him in the nets.

Before the start of the 1928–29 season, Chabot was sent to the Toronto Maple Leafs in return for goaltender John Ross Roach. Although Chabot had a career-low goals-against average of 1.61, the Toronto Maple Leafs did not make an impact in the regular season and in the playoffs until the 1931–32 season. Chabot was stellar in nets for the Leafs as they easily defeated the Chicago Blackhawks, and he held off the Maroons long enough for his team to score an overtime goal to send them into the finals for the first time since they last won the Cup as the Toronto St. Patricks in 1922. Playing against his former teammates, the New York Rangers, and the man he was traded for, John Ross Roach, Chabot proved to be the better goaltender in a high-scoring final as Toronto swept the best-of-five series in three games.

However, a steady job and some respect for his obvious talents seemed to evade the now-veteran netminder. He was again traded before the start of the 1933–34 season to the Montréal Canadiens for goaltender Georges Hainsworth. After seven seasons with Hainsworth, the Canadiens wanted to put a French Canadian goaltender between the pipes to appease the demanding Montréal fans. However, after just one season with the Habs, Chabot was on the move again, this time to the Chicago Blackhawks, who needed someone to replace Charlie Gardiner, who had died suddenly of a brain hemorrhage.

With Chicago, Chabot secured himself the Vezina Trophy after finishing first overall among the goaltenders with 88 goals-against for an average of 1.80. Luck never seemed to be on Chabot's side as the Blackhawks bowed out early in the playoffs to the tight defensive play of the Maroons and the goaltending of another legend, Alex Connell. The bad luck kept coming for Chabot. He suffered a knee injury that did not take him out for the season but was serious enough for the Blackhawks to replace him with backup Mike Karakas for the year. They sent Chabot off to the Montréal Maroons for the remainder of the 1935–36 season.

After he played just 16 regular season games with the team, the Maroons felt confident having veteran Chabot in goal for the first round of the playoffs against the Detroit Red Wings. In the first game of the series, Chabot and Red Wings goaltender Normie Smith battled to a scoreless tie by the end of the third period. Both teams had their chances on goal, but Chabot and Smith came close to standing on their heads to stop the barrage of pucks that came their way. The first overtime solved nothing. The second, third, fourth and fifth overtimes went by and still the two goaltenders stubbornly would not give up a goal. Unfortunately for Chabot, in the sixth overtime period Detroit's Mud Bruneteau ended the longest game ever to be played in the National Hockey League. That proved to be the nail in the coffin for the Maroons as the Red Wings went on to win their next two games to sweep the best-of-five series.

The playoff loss also spelled the end to Chabot's legendary career. He was cut by the Maroons during the off-season and would only play in six games the following season with the New York Americans before announcing his retirement from the sport.

During his career, he never really garnered the respect he deserved for his goaltending. He has yet to be named to the Hockey Hall of Fame. Chabot died at the age of 46 of osteoarthritis and progressive nephritis, a gradual shutting down of the body and the kidneys. A sad way for one of the best goaltenders of his time to die after such a successful career.

Cecil "Tiny" Thompson

Tiny was a big man. His nickname was a reference to the diminutive goals-against average he posted as a minor league player in the United States and as a rookie with the Boston Bruins. The same season Georges Hainsworth set NHL records with 22 shutouts and a goals-against average of 0.92, rookie Tiny Thompson led the league in wins and came second in goals-against with an average of 1.15. Thompson owed his success to his large frame, his lightning-quick legs and the fastest glove hand in the league. He was strictly a stand-up goaltender during a time when many goaltenders were experimenting by dropping to their knees to make a save. Being a stand-up goaltender, Thompson learned to play the angles to perfection, and with such a large frame in comparison with many goaltenders of his day, his opponents had a difficult time putting pucks in the net.

After a banner year as the most outstanding rookie in the league, Thompson took his Boston

Bruins into the 1929 playoffs with a good chance that they could make it far, given his abilities in the net. The Bruins faced off against goal-tender Georges Hainsworth and the Montréal Canadiens in the first round of the playoffs. Predictably, the scoring was held to a minimum, but the Bruins came out on the top as Thompson out-played the veteran Hainsworth to advance to the finals against the New York Rangers. The Bruins played the series to defensive perfection. Thompson held the fort, only allowing one goal to win his first Stanley Cup.

Thompson spoke of his rookie Cup win in a 1976 interview with *Hockey Digest*. "When your team finished first and goes on to win the Stanley Cup in your rookie season, that's quite a thrill."

Like all goaltenders for the new 1929–30 NHL season, Thompson had to adjust his goaltending style because of the new rule allowing forward passing, which opened up the offensive aspect of the game. But the new changes mattered little as Thompson led the league in goals-against average with 2.19 and in wins as the Bruins dominated the regular season with a record of 38–5–1.

Noting his instant success in the league and not wanting to hurt his chances, he decided to give up his favorite pastime: reading. "After all, the only thing a goaltender has is his eyes," Thompson once said famously.

Thompson continued his stellar play with the Bruins, but they could never seem to get anywhere in the playoffs after their victory in 1929. Still, over the next few years, Thompson added a few marks of prestige to his record. On April 3, 1933, Thompson and his Bruins battled the Toronto Maple Leafs in the second-longest game in NHL history. In the fifth and deciding match of the series, the game pushed into its sixth overtime period as Thompson and Leaf's goaltender Lorne Chabot held the fort for their exhausted teammates. The game seemed like it was going to go on forever, and it was even suggested that the series be decided by the simple flip of a coin. But the game continued, and finally the Leafs' Ken Doraty put the puck past an utterly exhausted Thompson after 104 minutes and 46 seconds of overtime play. The game did not end the way Thompson would have wanted, but he still put in a performance that no one could find fault with.

During the 1935–36 season, Thompson's strength and skill at handling the puck gave him another credit to his name. He became the first-ever goaltender to earn an assist when he fed a pass up ice to defenceman Babe Siebert, who then scored a goal against Toronto's George Hainsworth on January 14, 1936.

Thompson was a four-time winner of the Vezina Trophy: a record that would not be beaten until Bill Durnan won five. But for every athlete who reaches the top of his or her profession, it has to come to an end at some point to make room for the next generation of superstars.

After 11 seasons with the Bruins, Thompson was forced to sit out two games because of an eye problem. Bruins chief Art Ross decided to give a young American goaltender by the name of Frank Brimsek a chance in the Boston net. He played well, and when Thompson returned, he found himself on his way to Detroit. Thompson played two seasons with the Red Wings and a handful of games in the American Hockey League before announcing his retirement from the game he loved so much. He was inducted into the Hockey Hall of Fame in 1959. Even during retirement he could not leave hockey. Thompson became a scout for the Chicago Blackhawks and recruited a new generation of players to follow in his footsteps.

Roy "Shrimp" Worters

At only 5'3" and 135 pounds, Roy Worters was fittingly dubbed "Shrimp" early on in his career. He might be the smallest goaltender ever to play the position, but his ability on the ice made him seem like a giant to any opposition shooter who broke in on his net. With such a small stature in a game of large men, Worters quickly developed an attitude that size was unimportant when it came to playing his position. He always contested that if a goaltender played his angles right and came out to challenge a shooter then it wouldn't matter if he were 5'3" or 6' tall.

In the beginning of his career, it was difficult for Worters to find a team that would accept such a small goaltender. After a few years of trying in his native city of Toronto, he headed south to the United States Amateur Hockey Association with the Pittsburgh Yellow Jackets, where he led the league in all categories and quickly developed a fan following. When the NHL expanded for the 1925–26 season and the Pittsburgh Pirates franchise was looking for a goaltender, the management immediately thought of no one other than Roy Worters to lead the new team in their inaugural year in the National Hockey League.

In just his first season with his new NHL club, he helped them into third place overall and was second among the leading goaltenders, behind Alex Connell of the dominant Ottawa Senators.

The Pittsburgh Pirates had little hope against the Montréal Maroons in the NHL semifinals because of their weak defense and lack of scoring, but Roy Worters kept the series close and gave his team a chance to win, even though they lost in the end. Worters never minded the heavy workload dealt out to goaltenders on expansion teams. In one game, Worters stopped 70 of 73 shots in a 3–1 loss to the New York Americans.

Worters spent three seasons with the Pirates before a contract dispute sent him packing to the New York Americans, where he would play out the rest of his professional career. Although he only led the Americans into two playoffs, his coaches never questioned him when it came to his performance on the ice. Worters was unfortunately the goaltender for mediocre teams during his entire career.

In his first season with the New York Americans, Worters finished the season with a 1.15 goals-against average and 13 shutouts, but in the playoffs, his teammates could not score a single goal in a two-game total-goal series that they lost to the New York Rangers 1–0. Worters led the league with a 1.61 goals-against average during the 1930–31 regular season campaign, only letting in 74 goals. His teammates could only manage to score a pathetic 76 goals, making each of their wins close affairs with a lot of pressure on Worters to make the key saves to preserve each victory.

That kind of pressure gave Worters one of the greatest work ethics in the game. He was so tough that when he was hit by a Charlie Conacher slapshot in the throat, rather than falling to the ice and demanding medical attention, he held himself up by leaning on the crossbar and played out the rest of the game. His throat was so swollen from the hit that he wasn't able to eat solid food for two weeks, but he got the job done.

Worters played every game with the same intensity, even though he played for two teams that never made it into the Stanley Cup finals. Although he played just 11 playoffs games, he is remembered as one of the best goaltenders of his day. He retired from the game after the 1936–37 season in which he received some 200 stitches in his face and countless other injuries. The little guy from Toronto seemed invincible, but he lost a valiant battle with throat cancer in 1957. Worters was posthumously inducted into the Hockey Hall of Fame in 1969.

Walter "Turk" Broda

Walter Broda had an abundance of the one essential ingredient all goaltenders must possess: nerves of steel. As a child, he was smaller than most of his friends, and like most goaltenders, Broda was forced to play in nets rather than playing up front like he wanted. It was the best thing that could have happened to the young player. Along the way, honing his skills with his friends on the streets and frozen ponds, Broda picked up the nickname that would stick with him the rest of his life. Whenever he overexerted himself or became angry, his neck turned a bright red. One of his friends exclaimed, "Look at the turkey neck!" From then on, he was known as "Turk."

Later in life, after putting in his time in the minors, Broda got his first professional assignment with the Detroit Olympics of the International Hockey League. In Detroit, Broda began to turn the heads of some high-powered NHL men. Broda's break into the NHL came on a night when his Detroit team was to meet up against their rivals from the town of Windsor across Lake Erie. Toronto Maple Leafs general manager Conn Smythe was at the game to scout Windsor goaltender Eric Dickerson, whom

Smythe thought would be the perfect replacement for the veteran Georges Hainsworth. Unfortunately for Dickerson, he had an off night, and by the end of the third period, he had let in 8 goals. At the other end of the ice, Broda put on a goaltending clinic, stopping all shots that came his way for the shutout. Smythe immediately laid down a contract for Broda, and the following season, he was a member of the Toronto Maple Leafs. Detroit Red Wings coach Jack Adams knew about Broda from the goalie's days with the Olympics and assured Smythe he was a quality goaltender. "Broda hasn't a nerve in his body," declared Adams. "He could tend goal in a tornado and never blink an eye!"

Broda struggled initially under Dick Irvin's coaching. He took the team into the Stanley Cup finals in just his second year in the NHL, but he wasn't yet the goaltender Toronto fans would come to love. Broda would not reach his full potential until charismatic coach Hap Day was brought on board.

Working closely with Broda, Day focused on increasing the goaltender's speed and reducing his ever-expanding waistline. Broda improved so much that he shot up to fourth overall among the leading goaltenders and went straight to the top by the end of the 1940–41 season, winning the Vezina Trophy for his efforts. But the Boston

Bruins eliminated the Leafs in the opening round of the playoffs in a tough seven-game series.

Broda got another chance at the Stanley Cup the next year after a strong regular season. The Leafs finished in second place in the league, just 3 points behind the league-leading New York Rangers. Broda was inspiring in nets as the Leafs dispensed with the Rangers in six games and went on to meet the Detroit Red Wings in one of the most exciting finals in Stanley Cup history.

In the first three games of the finals against Detroit, the Leafs looked tired and battle-weary from the physical pounding. Broda did every-thing he could to keep the games level, but by the end of the third game, his team was staring at a 3–0 series deficit and a quick trip to the golf course if things didn't turn around. Hap Day benched a few of the regular players to stir things up. In doing, he so completely changed the out-come of the series.

Broda tightened things up in goal and the Leafs won the next four games straight. Broda had his first Cup, and the Leafs had established themselves as one of the dominant forces in the league during the 1940s. But in 1943, Broda took a leave from his duties on the ice and did a two-year tour of duty with the Canadian Armed Forces during World War II. He never saw any action and ended up playing on the armed forces hockey team most of the time. When Broda returned from Europe in 1945, he immediately resumed practicing with the Leafs.

Broda fell right back into the routine of NHL life and was quickly back to winning games for the Maple Leafs. He played 15 games for the Leafs at the end of the 1945–46 season but could not help them out of their losing slump. They missed the playoffs for the first time since 1930. However, for the 1946–47 season, Broda was back at the top of his game. All the players who had left to join in the war effort had resumed their regular spots, helping the Leafs to a second-place finish, just a few points behind the Montréal Canadiens. Fourth-place Detroit had little chance against Broda's goaltending and the offensive power of Toronto's Ted Kennedy and Syl Apps, losing the seven-game series in five. Montréal fared a little better with the goaltending of Vezina Trophy-winner Bill Durnan, but the Leafs were just too strong and Broda just too solid for the Canadiens. The Leafs won another Cup under Broda's protection and went on to win two more in 1948 and 1949 before the Detroit Red Wings rose to power under the blades of Ted Lindsay, Gordie Howe and Sid Abel. But Broda still had some tricks left in his repertoire before he considered retiring from the game.

With guys like Maurice Richard, Gordie Howe, and Sid Abel scoring at unprecedented rates, it was difficult for a goaltender to keep his goals-against average at a decent level, but with all these challenges Broda managed to stay competitive and keep his team in almost every game they played. With his help, the Leafs managed a respectable second place in the league standings by the end of the regular season. Broda could always be relied on to play a good game in the regular season, but it was under the extreme pressures of the playoffs that he really shone.

In the playoffs, Toronto easily took care of the Boston Bruins in five games, and Broda never let in more than 2 goals in any of them. In the finals, the Leafs met the Montréal Canadiens in one of the most legendary series ever played in NHL history.

Both the Leafs and the Canadiens played inspired hockey. Broda and Canadiens netminder Gerry McNeil made countless acrobatic saves to keep their teams in he competition. The teams were so evenly matched that every single game went into overtime, but by the fifth game the Leafs led the series three games to one and had the Canadiens on the ropes. The story was no different for the fifth game. McNeil and Broda were absolutely outstanding through three periods going into overtime with the score set in stone at two all. Just two minutes into overtime, a mad scramble developed in front of the Canadiens net, and Leafs defenseman Bill Barilko scored the Stanley Cup–winning goal.

"I couldn't beat him. Toe Blake couldn't. None of the Canadiens could," said Maurice Richard after the game.

That was Turk Broda's last Stanley Cup and his last year in the National Hockey League. He played one more game during the next season then hung up his pads for good. Broda was honoured with a special night at Maple Leafs Gardens where all the players and management from Toronto, the Bruins (whom they played that night), and every other NHL team came together to recognize one of the greatest players of their time. Turk received the ultimate honour when he was inducted into the Hockey Hall of Fame in 1967.

Frank Brimsek

Few other American-born players before Frank Brimsek were considered great. NHL hockey was largely a Canadian affair before the 1950s and had not really gained popularity as quickly in the U.S. as it had in Canada.

Hailing from the town of Eveleth, Minnesota, (a little community that can brag about producing quality goaltenders after sending the likes of Mike Karakas and Sam LoPresti all the way to the NHL), Brimsek got his professional start with teams such as the Pittsburgh Yellow Jackets, Providence Reds and the New Haven Eagles. He finally got his biggest challenge yet—number-one goaltender with the Boston Bruins. It wasn't the easiest position to fill. He was anointed the great replacement to Boston's favorite goaltender, Cecil "Tiny" Thompson, who had just come off a Vezina Trophy–winning season in 1938. Despite some initial criticism toward Boston's changing of the guard, Frank Brimsek quickly won everyone over with his spectacular saves and lightning-quick reflexes. He too finished the 1938–39 season with a Vezina Trophy to call his own and the best win record in the NHL with 36 wins and only 10 losses. Brimsek had a goals-against average of

1.56 and his closest competitor Dave Kerr of the Rangers had an average of 2.12. Brimsek also got to raise the Stanley Cup over his head when he put in an inspiring performance in the finals against the Toronto Maple Leafs. He even earned the Calder Trophy as rookie of the year. Not bad for a kid from the United States.

His cool, laid-back attitude on the ice fooled many shooters who though that Brimsek was playing his position lazily. They soon found out that he snapped to attention once they crossed into his zone. He was definitely a stand-up goaltender, but he would never shy away from the spectacular sprawling saves and was never one to avoid bruising the ankles of anyone who stepped into his way. He was so good that the Bruins remained the top team in the regular season for three years straight, and in 1941, he led his teammates back to the Promised Land—the Stanley Cup finals. After beating Turk Broda and the Maple Leafs in the opening round of the playoffs, Brimsek led his team into the finals against the Detroit Red Wings and promptly disposed of them in four games straight for the Bruins' second Stanley Cup in three years.

But Brimsek would have to give up on his National Hockey League dreams for a time while he did a tour of duty with the American Coast Guard and the military. Although the Bruins never won another Cup with Brimsek as their goaltender, on his return, he did help bring back the struggling Bruins who had lost some of their best players due to the war effort.

By 1949, the Bruins were no longer the team that they were before the war changed the power structure in the league. The Toronto Maple Leafs were at the top, and the Montréal Canadiens squad was getting better and better with each passing year. Needing a change, the Bruins sent Brimsek to the struggling Blackhawks, where the mediocre team pulled Brimsek into their losing ways. He retired just one season later, in 1950, before things got any worse. The goalie got his recognition in the Hockey Hall of Fame in 1966.

Long-time friend and former teammate Milt Schmidt described Brimsek's legacy in comparison to the best goaltenders of all time. "When Brimmy played with the Boston Bruins, he was in my opinion the best of the goaltenders, and that takes in a lot of territory. I thought he was better than Sawchuk."

Bill Durnan

Spending just seven years in the National Hockey League, Bill Durnan packed a career's worth of recognition into that short period of time. Durnan won the Vezina Trophy an incredible six times, a feat only one other goaltender in National Hockey League history accomplished— Jacques Plante—and he added some more silverware to his mantle piece with two Stanley Cup championships.

A natural athlete, during his amateur days he played hockey in the winter and baseball in the summer, but it was hockey that he loved the most. Durnan learned one of his most important and unique assets early on in his career from a minor league coach who taught him to be able to use either hand for catching and blocking, making the goalie completely ambidextrous. But stardom did not come immediately for Durnan, who ended up languishing in the juniors for several years before finally being noticed by Canadiens manager Tommy Gorman. Durnan played in his first NHL game at the age of 28—old for any professional athlete—but Durnan played like he was 20.

After 13 seasons without a Stanley Cup, the Canadiens were happy to begin the 1943–44 season with the services of a goaltender of Durnan's caliber. It also didn't hurt that the Canadiens had the high scoring trio of Maurice Richard, Toe Blake, and Elmer Lach (the players also known as the "Punch Line") on the ice for the first time.

Durnan led the league in his rookie season in wins and goals-against, taking home the Vezina Trophy for his efforts and becoming the first rookie to win the award. Playing the full 50-game schedule, Durnan had a goals-against average of 2.18. The closest record of any goaltender to play the full 50 games was sixth place Rangers goaltender Ken McAuley, who had an average of 6.24. Durnan continued his regular season heroics into the post-season taking the Canadiens past the Toronto Maple Leafs in the first round, when he only let in three goals in the first game and no more than one for the remainder of the series. In the Stanley Cup finals it was another easy time for the Canadiens against the Chicago Blackhawks as Durnan kept them off the score board and the forwards did the job up front, burying the Hawks in four straight games to win the Stanley Cup.

Durnan would add three more Vezina Trophies to his collection and another Stanley Cup by 1946, earning a secure place among the best goaltenders in league history in an incredibly short time. Except for one year, in 1947–48, when the Canadiens failed to make the playoffs and he slipped down to third overall among the leading goaltenders, Durnan was the best at his profession. But the pressures of winning, especially in a city like Montréal, started to eat away at Durnan's nerves.

"It got so bad that I couldn't sleep on the night before a game," said Durnan. "I couldn't even keep my meals down."

Although he was always a calm and cool character on the ice, even his teammates began to notice that the pressures of the game's most difficult position were starting to wear on Durnan's nerves.

Teammate Ken Reardon recalled one moment of stress in Kevin Allen's book, *Without Fear*. "When he was with us in the dressing room and off the ice, he was an easy-going guy. But we had this anteroom off of the dressing room, and during games, the only one allowed in there between periods was Bill. He'd be in there, smoking a cigarette. That was where he found his solace from the game, his solitude."

Durnan tried not to let the pressures of the game get to him because the last thing he wanted to do was to let his teammates and the city down, but his nerves could not cope with the stress. After another Vezina Trophy–winning season, he announced his retirement at the age of 35. The Canadiens would not see another goaltender like him until Jacques Plante came along in 1953. Durnan was inducted into Hall of Fame in 1964.

Terry Sawchuck

While he was arguably the best goaltender in National Hockey League history, Terry Sawchuk's successes on the ice were often overshadowed by his tribulations off the ice. From early on in his life, Sawchuk went through many ups and downs before he even made it into the pros.

Sawchuk got into hockey when his older brother Mike helped coach him through his first few difficult steps into the goaltending world.

Terry faced the first tragedy of his life when his brother died suddenly of a heart murmur. Sawchuk also lost his other older brother, Roger, to pneumonia later on. These tragedies were difficult for a teenager to deal with. Using them as motivation, Sawchuk built himself into one of the best goaltenders around before finally getting his big break in the NHL.

During Sawchuk's first year in the American Hockey League (AHL), he ended up taking home the rookie of the year award in 1949 after winning the award in the United States Hockey League (USHL) just one year earlier.

In those years in the American hockey system, Sawchuk began a long list of injuries that would plague him his entire life. As a kid, he had suffered a broken right arm that needed several operations and healed four centimetres shorter than his left. Playing with the Omaha Knights of the USHL, Sawchuk nearly had his career ended prematurely when he received three stitches to his eye for an injury caused by an errant stick. His elbow was a constant source of pain, irritated by bone chips resulting from the constant smacking on the ice to make a save. Despite Sawchuk's long list of problems Detroit Red Wings' management knew that they had to take a chance on Sawchuk because he was just too good to pass up even with his injuries.

Sawchuk was originally in the Boston Bruins farm system, but he was traded to Detroit before he ever played a single game in the NHL, something Boston almost certainly regretted later. His entrance into the big league came at the end of the 1949–50 season. Detroit's regular goaltender Harry Lumley was out with an injury for several games, and Sawchuk got the nod that he would take his place. In just seven games, Sawchuk made enough of an impression with the Red Wings management to earn his place as Detroit's number-one goaltender.

After seeing Sawchuk's display of goaltending prowess in those seven games New York Rangers coach Lynn Patrick had some lofty words of praise for the minor-league goalie. "There are three big-league goalies in hockey, and one of them is in the minors."

In his first full season as the Red Wings number-one goaltender, Sawchuk played the full 70-game schedule, led the league in wins with 44, took home the Calder Trophy as the rookie of the year, and should have won the Vezina Trophy with a goals-against average of 1.99. The Vezina was given to Al Rollins instead, who had a lower average but played 30 fewer games.

Sawchuk's unique style of goaltending was one of the main reasons for his initial successes. While most goaltenders of his time preferred a straight stand-up style, Sawchuk crouched low to the ice so he could see the puck, allowing him to use his explosive speed to make saves rather than relying on positioning himself squarely with the shooter each time. His whole style seemed to rely on an unending supply of pent-up energy that he used to shout at teammates, confront people in the stadium, dive, scramble and make some spectacular saves. Effective, yes, but his style left him open to injuries as well as the inevitable stresses that all goaltenders feel.

Because he crouched low to the ice, his upper body and face were open to any errant sticks, pucks, skates and fists that might come his way. Over his career guarding a hockey net, Terry Sawchuk received over 400 stitches to the face and suffered countless problems with his back, several missing teeth and numerous broken bones. Add that to a long hospital list of aliments and injuries, and you have a life lived on the edge. As a regular Joe Citizen, Sawchuk punctured a lung in a car accident and had to undergo an emergency appendectomy. On top of that, the stress of the most pressure-filled job in hockey and a fiery temper were all the ingredients for man who walked on the darker side of life.

Sawchuk simply focused on the next game and on the next save to get away from everything.

For his sophomore season with the Wings, Sawchuk finished with a Vezina Trophy-winning 1.90 goals-against average and another 44 wins. Detroit was riding high with a first-place finish and a full head of steam going into the first round of the playoffs against the Toronto Maple Leafs. Sawchuk dominated the play with two shutouts and only three goals allowed in the Wings' four-game sweep of the series. Sawchuk did the same to the Montréal Canadiens, only allowing two goals in the first two games and shutting them out in the final two as the Wings swept their way to the Stanley Cup. Sawchuk finished with a goals-against average of 0.63 and a place in the pantheon of great goaltenders. Sawchuk helped the Red Wings to two more titles by 1955 and was still at the peak of his game five years into his professional NHL career.

Things all began to change when one night against the Boston Bruins, Sawchuk let in 8 goals and was given a few games off to relax and get his mind off hockey. Rookie goaltender Glenn Hall was brought in from the minors to fill in and did so well that Detroit traded Sawchuk to the Boston Bruins along with eight other players in a massive deal. It was the beginning of some more hard times for the all-star goaltender.

Sawchuk's desire to win in Boston simply wasn't there, and the gritty netminder quickly went from top of the league down to the bottom along with the basement-dwelling Bruins. In his second season in Boston, Sawchuk fell into a depression and talked about retiring from the game. Things weren't going well with his wife, and he wanted to be closer to his family. Then, just two years after leaving the Red Wings, Sawchuk convinced Detroit's management to trade Hall to Chicago and let Sawchuk take his place back between the Red Wings goal posts.

But the team Sawchuk returned to was no longer the same one he had left. Detroit had lost a few players, and they just did not seem to have the chemistry they had when they dominated the league in the early '50s. Still, the management stuck with their veteran goaltender, and the fiery Sawchuk proved to them that he still had what it took to be one of the best goaltenders in the NHL. While Detroit had two mediocre seasons in 1962–63 and 1963–64, they did very well in the playoffs, almost entirely thanks to Terry Sawchuk's skills. Though they did not win the Cup in those two years they made it to the finals both times because Sawchuk was always at his best when the pressure was on and the game meant something to his team. At the end of 1964, the Red Wings management was looking for a change in nets and decided to leave Sawchuk off its protected list of players. Toronto jumped at the chance and paired him up with another veteran goaltender, Johnny Bower.

At the end of Sawchuk's first regular season with the Maple Leafs, he and Johnny Bower shared the Vezina Trophy, bringing a renewed confidence to Sawchuk's game. In the 1966–67 Stanley Cup playoffs, Sawchuk's impact on the team was truly felt.

Without care for personal safety, Sawchuk threw himself in front of every shot the Chicago Blackhawks, his first-round opponents, could throw at him. Even Bobby Hull's blistering shot, which knocked Sawchuk out of the game for several minutes more than once, couldn't defeat the goalie. Each time, Sawchuk came back stronger and more determined.

"We started the period on a power play and I drilled a shot that hit him in the shoulder, and he lay on the ice for about 15 minutes. He got up and he was as loose as a goose," said a frustrated Hull in an interview with writer D'Arcy Jenish. "I had 11 shots on him and couldn't put a pea past him." Toronto beat the Blackhawks in six games and faced off against their Montréal arch-rivals for the last Stanley Cup of the original-six era. Although Sawchuk allowed 12 goals in two of the games, he played inspired hockey for the remainder of the series to give the Leafs 4–1 and 3–1 victories in the final two games as they upset the Canadiens to win the Stanley Cup.

After the 1967 Stanley Cup victory with the Maple Leafs, Sawchuk was left unprotected during the expansion draft and was picked up by the Los Angeles Kings. But after spending three more unsuccessful years with the Kings, going back to Detroit, and finally playing with the New York Rangers, things suddenly came to a tragic halt. Sawchuk was living separately from his wife, sinking into a depression, and frequently battled the effects of the bottle. During a fight with his roommate and teammate Ron Stewart over some money, Sawchuk injured himself and had to be rushed to the hospital. His gallbladder was removed and he received several operations on his lacerated liver. One month later, he died from his injuries. During his time in the hospital, Sawchuk completely absolved his friend Stewart of any wrong doing, placing the blame squarely on his own poor judgment. Just one year later, the normal three-year waiting period was waved, and Terry Sawchuk became a distinguished Hall of Fame member. Today, he is remembered more for the good he brought into the world than for the darkness that was always with him.

Jacques Plante

His eccentric character, odd behaviour in and out of the net and disregard for hockey convention and traditions were all key ingredient in making Jacques Plante one of the most influential goaltenders in NHL history.

Like many kids, from an early age Plante was always playing hockey whenever he could, but being a forward or a defenceman was never really his style. When he first strapped on a pair of leg pads, he fell in love with goaltending. After a few years of playing for a factory team, Plante moved his way up through the junior system in Québec City and was fortunate enough to get a spot on the Montréal Canadiens farm team, the Montréal Royals, in 1951. The Canadiens were a good team in 1951, but they needed a permanent replacement for Bill Durnan, who had set the goaltending bar so high that interim goaltender Gerry McNeil was having difficulties meeting such standards. Canadiens management was excited to try out the young prospect and brought him up from the farm team to test him out for a few games in 1952–53 and 1953–54. The team immediately decided to replace McNeil after Plante's performance in the 1954 playoff finals against Detroit. They lost the Cup that year to Detroit, but the Canadiens knew they had something special in Plante.

Special might not be the right word when describing Plante. Something more along the lines of eccentric would be the proper way to describe this giant of a character on and off the ice.

In his spare time during practices, Plante could be found knitting tuques to help him relax. As an asthmatic, his breathing problems often forced him to get separate hotel rooms or even hotels on away games. Not a popular move in such a group as close-knit as a professional hockey team, but on the ice, his focus was completely on the game.

Plante had another peculiar habit of wandering out of his net to play the puck during an era when most goaltenders stayed within the confines of the painted blue ice around the net. He developed this technique during his time in the Québec junior league when he was on a particularly bad team whose defensemen could not skate backwards and were generally inept at playing the puck. Plante had to get it himself to clear the zone. The more he did it, the farther he went out to play the puck. The strategy seemed to work, so he incorporated it into his game.

Plante used his unique style and his lightning reflexes to help turn the Montréal Canadiens of the late 1950s into one of the greatest hockey teams of all time. From 1956 to 1960, Jacques Plante led the Canadiens to four league championships and five consecutive Stanley Cup championships. He added five consecutive Vezina Trophies for his own personal collection. But one of Plante's most memorable contributions to the game during those years came during the first half of the 1959–60 season.

The famous moment in question came on November 1, 1959, when the Canadiens met the New York Rangers at Madison Square Garden. Some 30 years earlier, Clint Benedict of the Montréal Maroons was the first goaltender to break convention and wear a mask during a regular season game because of a broken nose. Regardless of the protection the mask could provide a goaltender, it failed to catch on. For another 30 years, goaltenders would go on bravely without concern for their safety. Times change, however, and with the advent of the slapshot, goaltenders began to reevaluate that tiny piece of protection. But NHL tradition and machismo dictated that goaltenders wear the mask. It took an eccentric character like Jacques Plante to break the norm.

During a game at Madison Square Garden, Rangers forward Andy Bathgate blasted a powerful shot that caught Plante in the nose, sending a gush of blood all over Plante's jersey and the ice. Plante was taken to the dressing room to be stitched up and was told by Canadiens head coach Toe Blake to get back out on the ice. Plante refused to return to active duty unless he could wear the mask that he used in practice. With no other goaltending option available, Blake relented and allowed Plante to reassume his position in the Canadiens' net. From that game on, Plante wore a mask until the day he retired from hockey. Soon other goaltenders followed, and by the 1970s, no goaltender went without the essential piece of hockey protection.

"Plante was the happiest guy in the rink that he got cut," said longtime Canadiens broadcaster Dick Irvin Jr. "Don't ever feel sorry for him because he was looking for the opportunity."

After the Canadiens incredible run of five consecutive Stanley Cups, the chemistry that held the team together through those years began to break apart. Maurice Richard retired in 1960, Doug Harvey was traded to the New York Rangers and other teams like Chicago and Toronto were finally winning in the playoffs. By the end of the 1962–63 season, the Canadiens wanted a change in the Montréal net and traded Plante to the New York Rangers in return for Lorne "Gump" Worsley.

Things did not go that well for Plante with his new team. After two seasons of suffering from health problems and several poor performances he was sent down to the minors to regain his form. Plante did not return the next season, preferring retirement to spending another season languishing in the minors.

Money brought Plante out of retirement in 1968, when the expansion St. Louis Blues offered the 39-year-old goaltender $35,000 (or more) to return to his place between the pipes.

Plante was teamed up with veteran Glenn Hall. The two Hall of Fame goaltenders won the Vezina Trophy with the fewest goals-against and took their team all the way to the Stanley Cup finals against Plante's former team, the Montréal Canadiens, but they were outmatched in the finals and lost in four straight games. Plante was traded to the Toronto Maple Leafs for the 1970–71 season, where he finished with the best goals-against average in the league with 1.88 but saw an early exit in the playoffs. Plante played another season with Toronto, a few games in Boston and one season with the Edmonton Oilers of the World Hockey Association before finally calling it quits in 1975.

The eclectic man of the world moved to Switzerland to live in peace after his retirement. He died of stomach cancer in 1986 at the age of 57.

Glenn "Mr. Goalie" Hall

While goaltenders such as Plante and Sawchuk brought a fiery, dynamic approach to the game, Glenn Hall played the position to technical perfection. "Mr. Goalie," as he was called, earned his place in the pros by working his way up through Saskatchewan then into the Detroit farm system before ousting legendary Red Wings goaltender Terry Sawchuk in 1955 as that team's number one. Not a bad accomplishment considering Sawchuk was in his prime and had just come off a Stanley Cup– and Vezina Trophy–winning season.

Detroit was confident they could go far with the young goaltender who played the game like no other before him. Sawchuk was breaking the mold of the stand-up goaltender, but Hall completely tore it apart with his unique way of dropping to his knees while spreading his legs towards the far corners of the net in what is known today as the butterfly style. From his low stance on the ice, he had a better view of shots from the blue line and could make the occasional acrobatic save much easier. His style at the time drew many critics, but it is the norm among top NHL goaltenders today.

Hall played inspired hockey in his first year, taking home the Calder Trophy as the top rookie, but he could not get his teammates past the Montréal Canadiens in the finals to win the 1956 Stanley Cup. Although Hall led the Wings to the top of the league standings at the end of the 1956–57 regular season, coach Jack Adams did not like the way Hall performed in the play-offs, and he traded his goaltender to Chicago along with teammate Ted Lindsay.

In Chicago, Hall continued his streak of playing in every single game. The Blackhawks were still not the powerful offensive team that they would become in the '60s, but Hall held the fort until 1961 when the Hawks stopped Montréal's consecutive Cup wins at five during the opening round of the playoffs.

After four games of the Montréal-Chicago series, the teams were tied up at two games apiece. In the fifth game, Hall took control of the series and put his team in a good position with a 3–0 shutout. At that point, the Canadiens were utterly defeated. Hall posted another 3–0 shutout to upset the Canadiens and put Chicago in contention for the Stanley Cup for the first time since 1944.

Detroit had little chance against the Hawks with Hall playing some of the best clutch hockey in his career, allowing the Red Wings to score no more than three goals in one game. The Hawks took the series in six games and won their first Stanley Cup since 1938 (and, as of 2006, their last).

Hall continued his incredible streak of consecutive games into the 1962–63 season, up until the 552nd game. Hall had played numerous games injured with cuts, pulled muscles and even a concussion, but he never would have expected to end his streak the way he did on November 8, 1963. While getting dressed for the game that night, he bent over to adjust a strap on his leg pad and pulled something in his back. Hall tried to walk off the strain, but the pain was just too great, and his amazing streak came to an end.

Hall played several more successful seasons with Chicago, winning the Vezina Trophy in 1967 (shared with Dennis Dejordy). At the 1967 expansion draft, Hall was left unprotected and was picked up by the St. Louis Blues. Thanks to Hall's outstanding performance in front of a mediocre expansion team, the Blues made it to three consecutive Stanley Cup finals, unfortunately losing each one to the more powerful established Eastern League teams. In those three years, Hall took home the Conn Smythe Trophy in 1968 for his efforts in getting the team so far into the playoffs and shared the Vezina Trophy in 1969 with fellow legend Jacques Plante. But by 1970–71, the pressure of playing the game was starting to wear him down.

The off-season was an important time for Hall. He liked to work on his farm and take life easy, getting away from all the stresses of professional hockey. Throughout his career, game time meant speeding pucks, important saves, cuts, injuries, pressure—all things that put him on edge and made him nervous, so much so that he often threw up before each game. Teammates joked that the bucket beside his locker should be enshrined in the Hockey Hall of Fame.

At the end of the 1970–71 season, Hall brought an end to his illustrious 16-year NHL career. He did not leave hockey completely but worked as a goaltending consultant for a few years. Hall could now relax and focus on the things that didn't make him sick. He was inducted into the Hockey Hall of Fame in 1975. For a goaltender who described a hockey game as "60 minutes of hell!" he carved out one of the most legendary careers in the NHL history.

Al Rollins

If there was a trophy given at the end of the regular season for the player who put in the most effort, it would have surely gone to goaltender Al Rollins for his dismal years spent in Chicago. Luckily, his career didn't start out that way.

Signed into the Toronto Maple Leafs farm system, Rollins finally got his chance in the big leagues in 1949, taking the place of the injured Turk Broda for two games. Conn Smythe was pleased with his slender 6'2" frame and ability to maintain focus in an environment hostile to someone replacing the popular Broda. Rollins impressed Smythe enough to earn a regular spot on the team for the 1950–51 season playing in 40 regular season games earning a goals-against average of 1.77, which won him the Vezina Trophy and his first chance at a run for the Stanley Cup. Splitting duties with Broda, Rollins played in four playoff games and helped the Leafs win the Stanley Cup. When Broda retired that summer, the Toronto netminder's job was Rollins' for the taking.

After having a fantastic 1951–52 season, coming in second behind Terry Sawchuk in the leading goaltenders with 2.22 goals-against compared to Sawchuk's 1.90, Rollins saw his team into the post-season.

But goaltenders live and die in the playoffs, and after the Leafs bowed out in the first round to the Detroit Red Wings in four games, it was Rollins' time to face the trading block. Conn Smythe felt a shake up was needed in his team and traded Rollins for Chicago Blackhawks goaltender Harry Lumley. Although Lumley won the Vezina Trophy in 1954, the trade benefited neither of the clubs as Chicago spent the '50s in the cellar of the league, and Toronto could find no luck in the playoffs. The Blackhawks were so bad that in the 1953–54 season, they only won 12 games, losing 51. Every game, Rollins faced impossible odds as the team in front of him let the opponents have free run of the ice. If not for Rollins' stellar goaltending, the Hawks would have struggled to hit the double-digit mark in wins. His 3.23 goals-against average and last place finish was by no means a reflection on his effectiveness as a goaltender, which is why the National Hockey League awarded him the Hart Trophy as the most valuable player despite his losing record.

Rollins was fighting a losing battle. The Blackhawks had the worst record in the NHL for four out of five years that Rollins played on the team. After another losing season in 1956–57, Rollins retired from the game. Frustrated at being on a losing team for so long, Rollins chose obscurity rather than waiting for a trade to change his career. Although he played 10 games for the New York Rangers in 1959–60, Rollins hung up his pads for good and let history decide where he stands among the great goaltenders of all time.

Roger Crozier

Roger Crozier was an average-size goaltender, but he was blessed with incredible reflexes, lateral speed, and one of the fastest glove hands in the NHL. But like Glenn Hall, Crozier was plagued by the stresses of the game to the point where it began to affect his health. Still, he was able to shrug off most of the pain in his life and play the game he loved to perfection.

In his first full season with Detroit, replacing the legendary Terry Sawchuk, Crozier impressed his team well enough to play in all 70 games during the 1964–65 season. He was the last goaltender in NHL history to play in all his team's games in one season and take home the Calder Trophy as the league's top rookie.

Crozier continued to impress in his sophomore season, finishing the regular season with a respectable 2.78 goals-against average, but during the playoffs, Crozier's magic truly shined. He out-dueled the Chicago Blackhawks' Glenn Hall in the playoffs' opening round and kept his outplayed Red Wings alive until the sixth game of the Stanley Cup finals against the Montréal Canadiens. Although he lost the Cup to the Canadiens, Crozier was honoured with the Conn Smythe Trophy as the playoff's most valuable player for his superhuman efforts in nets for the Red Wings.

His efforts were all the more astonishing given that Crozier was fighting severe ulcers and pancreatitis. With a goaltender of his caliber, you have to wonder just what he might have been able to accomplish if he were healthy throughout his career. Keeping his weight above 160 pounds was often a challenge. At the age of 25 he was stressed to such a degree that he lost confidence in his abilities and retired from the game. After spending four months in his hometown working part time as a carpenter, Crozier returned to the NHL, but was never able to shake the reputation as a nervous, unstable goaltender.

Detroit wanted a more stable goaltender and dealt Crozier to the expansion Buffalo Sabres in 1970. In the beginning, things did not go well for Crozier. Finally, after two losing seasons, Crozier posted a winning record in the 1972–73 season. But again, health problems kept him from fully contributing to the success of the team. After more than 30 trips to the hospital because of his pancreatitis, Crozier retired from the game for good in 1977.

His Buffalo goaltending partner, Dave Dryden, spoke of Crozier's philosophical approach to the game in Kevin Allen's book *Without Fear*. "I did get a kick out of his philosophy. He was always saying when he was up in Bracebridge [his hometown], on the roof of a cottage and hammering a nail, that there aren't 15,000 people booing if he bends one. If you bend a nail, you bend a nail. He would hint that he couldn't take the pressure."

Crozier stayed in hockey after his retirement, serving in the front office of the Washington Capitals for several years. He even served as the Capitals' general manager for a brief period. Under his watch, the team selected Scott Stevens during the 1982 draft.

Crozier's illnesses finally got the better of him in 1996 when he died after a fight with cancer.

The National Hockey League unveiled the Roger Crozier Saving Grace Award in 2000, which is given annually to the goaltender with the best save percentage.

Chapter Three

THE MODERN ERA (1967–PRESENT)

Tony Esposito

It was never easy for him to be second to his brother Phil, but after just one full season in the National Hockey League, people started looking at Tony Esposito in a whole new light.

Tony Esposito began as a goaltender because his older brother needed someone to score goals on in their hometown of Sault Ste. Marie. Little did they realize at the time that one day they would face off against each other as the most successful brother combination in NHL.

While brother Phil had been burning up the league since 1963, it wasn't until 1969 that his little brother Tony got his first shot with the big boys playing for the Montréal Canadiens. The Canadiens had lost both their regular goaltenders to injuries and called upon their young farm team goalie to help stop the gap left by the injured veterans. As if fate had planned it, Tony's first full NHL assignment came on December 5, 1968, against the Boston Bruins and his brother Phil at the Boston Garden. Tony played an inspiring game except for two goals that he allowed his brother Phil to score. The final score was a 2–2 tie.

Tony later recalled in an interview in Kevin Allen's *Without Fear*, "Phil got both their goals. His little brother, making his first NHL start, and he shows me no pity."

Although he played excellent hockey for the Canadiens, he was moved to Chicago in an inter-league draft. It was rumoured that Canadiens general manager Sam Pollock owed Hawks General Manager Tommy Ivan a favour and see-ing that the Hawks were sitting in last place it would not do any harm to send Tony to Chicago. Pollock quickly regretted sending the goaltender off to the Hawks so easily. In his first full season with Chicago, Esposito took the Hawks out of the basement straight to the top of the league, just ahead of his brother's Boston Bruins. He won the Vezina and Calder Trophies for his spectacular play and recorded an incredible 15 shutouts all in his rookie season. But Tony would not get a chance at the Stanley Cup that year. His brother and the Boston Bruins eliminated the Blackhawks in four games straight in the semifinals and eventually went on to win the Stanley Cup.

Esposito never backed down from a challenge and helped the Blackhawks to another successful season, finishing third overall in the league in 1971 and putting his team in a good position in the playoffs. They faced off against the Philadelphia Flyers in the opening round. Philadelphia could only muster a maximum of two goals per game against the solid Chicago netminder, and the Flyers were defeated in four games straight. The New York Rangers were a little tougher to beat, but Esposito managed to hold them off to make it into the final against his old teammates, the Montréal Canadiens.

The Canadiens were by far the stronger team, and they had Ken Dryden's sensational goaltending on their side. The Hawks still did not make it easy for Montréal taking it to the seventh game, which the Canadiens won by a score of 3–2.

Esposito and Dryden teamed up for the 1972 eight-game Summit Series against the Soviets in a tournament to decide which was the better hockey nation. Esposito's play was inspiring, keeping his team alive against the mighty Soviet squad, and he was a key ingredient in Canada's victory in the series.

Back in the NHL the next season, things continued to roll along for Esposito. Chicago dominated during the regular season, with

Esposito putting in another Vezina Trophy winning season in 1971–72, but he had no luck in the playoffs. The Hawks made it into the Stanley Cup final again in 1973, but they ran into a much tougher Montréal Canadiens squad this time around and were beaten in six games despite Esposito's valiant efforts.

Esposito played a style of game similar to that of his idol Glenn Hall. But Esposito changed the style a bit by playing more aggressively in his nets, often going into the butterfly position on every save. He wasn't a very large man at 5'11" and 185 pounds, but when he was in net with all his equipment on, he might as well have been 6'5" and 250 pounds—he was able to make himself that big in goal. Although extremely cool on the ice, Esposito was like most goaltenders and suffered from shaky nerves most of his career. On the night of a game, Esposito would not talk to anyone and would completely isolate himself from the team and even from his family. He always said that he needed the time to himself to get into the right mindset to have frozen pucks shot at him for 60 minutes.

The good times did not last forever. Chicago went through some lean years in the late '70s, and Esposito began to play fewer and fewer games. His goals-against average began to climb above the 3.00 mark, and by the 1982–83 season,

Esposito began pondering his retirement from the game.

"We had absolutely no desire to win," said Esposito of the bad days in Chicago in the late '70s. "The only desire was to survive, to get to your paycheck. The attitude was terrible, and I made up my mind that if it didn't change I wouldn't be back. I couldn't be associated with it anymore."

The kid brother of Phil Esposito was now the oldest player in the NHL at over 40 years of age. Just a few years back, he was listening to the wisdom of the veteran players. Now he found himself in the position of a leader, and he wasn't afraid to let the other players on the team know that he wasn't happy. He played 18 games but in the 1983–84 season was not making saves like he used to and had a goals-against average of 4.82, something he hadn't seen since the days his brother took shots on him back in their hometown. After the Hawks' early elimination from the 1984 playoffs, Esposito decided to hang up his pads for good. He didn't stay out of the game for long though, joining the Pittsburgh Penguins organization as director of hockey operations. He later worked with Phil in the front offices of the expansion Tampa Bay Lightning. Tony Esposito joined his brother in the Hockey Hall of Fame in 1988.

Gerry Cheevers

Unfortunately for Gerry Cheevers, he began his professional career during the 1960s, when the National Hockey League had just six teams and the chances for a rookie goaltender to earn a regular spot were slim. The odds were stacked against him even more given that the Toronto Maple Leafs owned his contract and the number-one goaltender's spot was very well filled by Johnny Bower. Cheevers only played two NHL games for the Leafs in 1961–62. Toronto had no need for a young goaltender and left him unprotected in an intra-league draft where the Boston Bruins picked him up. After two seasons of shuttling back and forth between the minors and the Bruins, Cheevers was brought on board as a fulltime employee in 1967–68.

Cheevers joined one of the most exciting offensive teams in the league in the late '60s as players like Bobby Orr and Phil Esposito rewrote the record books with their sheer ability to put pucks in the net. This offensive mindset was great for scoring, but while Cheevers' teammates were rushing up one end of the ice, he was left to fend off counterattacks that usually came in the form of odd-man rushes. But Cheevers never cared about letting in a few goals as long as his teammates scored more. Cheevers did not care about his average or save percentages—he had another goal in mind when it came to hockey. "Pride," said Cheevers. "I get it out of winning."

When it came time to make the big saves, his teammates always knew they could count on Cheevers to deliver. His style, however, left some of the coaches on the Bruins bench tearing their hair out. Like many goaltenders, who spend a career in one area of the ice, Cheevers liked to get out of the crease and roam around a little when the puck came near the net. He played lacrosse in the off-season and felt confident in his roaming and puck-handling skills, but on many occasions he was the victim of his own confidence. "I've made a fool out of myself more than once," Cheevers said.

Cheevers had another famous trademark that he started in his second season with the Bruins in 1968–69. Before joining the professional ranks, Cheevers never wore a hockey mask. But once a pro, he felt it was time to join the other goaltenders under a mask. Other goaltenders were satisfied with plain white fiberglass. Cheevers, always searching for new ways to be different, began painted stitches to indicate where the puck would have left a scar. He explained how the painting all got started in Andrew Podniek's book,

Kings of Ice. "I was trying to get out of practice one day when this shot that couldn't have broken an egg hit me in the mask. I faked a serious injury and went into the dressing room. I was sitting there having a Coke when Harry Sinden [the Bruins' coach] came in and told me to get back out onto the ice. All the guys were laughing, so I knew I had to do something. I told the trainer to paint a 30-stitch gash on the mask. Then I went out and told Harry, 'See how bad it is!'" After that day, with each puck that struck his mask he added another mark until it was covered in stitches, perfectly illustrating the necessity of the facemask. All jokes and criticisms aside, the Bruins knew that behind that scarred mask was a goaltender who knew how to win and could take Boston far into the playoffs.

In 1968 and 1969, the Montréal Canadiens eliminated the Bruins in the early rounds, but by the 1969–70 season, the Canadiens had fallen far behind the high-powered offence of the Bruins and failed to make the post-season for the first time since 1948. With the Canadiens out of the way, the Bruins dispensed with their first round opponents, the New York Rangers, in six games and easily moved past the Chicago Blackhawks in the semifinals in four straight. The Bruins were up against the St. Louis Blues in the final, but they provided little challenge as Boston swept the series in four straight games. Cheevers didn't have the best goals-against average or best save percentage that season, but he did have his first Stanley Cup, and that's all history would remember.

After another early exit in the playoffs in 1971 courtesy of the Montréal Canadiens, the Boston Bruins returned in the 1972 playoffs determined to carry their regular season success forward. Boston easily made it through the first two teams. They had a little trouble with the Rangers in the Stanley Cup finals, but Cheevers got a 3–0 shutout in the sixth game of the series to win his second Stanley Cup in three years.

Boston continued to flourish under Cheevers' watchful eye, but the late 1970s belonged to the Montréal Canadiens. On more than one occasion, the Canadiens dashed Cheevers' hopes of another Stanley Cup—in 1977, 1978 and 1979 to be exact. Now an old man by league standards and suffering from recurring knee problems, Cheevers decided to retire after the 1979–80 season.

Cheevers did not retire completely however. He accepted an offer to become head coach of the Boston Bruins after the departure of former coach Don Cherry. Cheevers coached the Bruins through several winning seasons but they never found any luck in the playoffs. In 1985, he retired from his tour of duty as a coach with a record of 204 wins and 126 losses and received his induction into the Hockey Hall of Fame in 1985.

Vladislav Tretiak

The world first got a good look at Tretiak at the 1972 Summit Series. Scouting reports all said that the Soviet goaltender was the weakest part of the team and suffered from inconsistent play and a weak glove hand. However, the scout who filed that report had only seen Tretiak play one game in which he let in nine goals. The 20-year-old Tretiak had seen action with the Soviets in the world championships and in the Olympics and had performed better than the scouting reports suggested.

Despite his confidence in Tretiak's ability to stop the Canadians in the Summit Series, one veteran goaltender thought the young Soviet could use a few tips on how to play against Canada's potent offence. Before the opening game in Montréal, Tretiak received a visitor in the Soviet dressing room. It was none other than goaltending legend Jacques Plante, and the first thing that he said to the young player was,

"Steady strain. That is the fate of us goaltenders."
Plante, who was known for keeping actual books
on the habits of the league's best shooters, gave
Tretiak a detailed account on how to play each
of Canada's best scorers. The tutorial seemed to
help as the Soviets went on to defeat Canada 7–3
in the opening game. After the game, Canada's
Peter Mahovlich said that Tretiak had played so
well and knew all his moves like he had known
him since he was a kid. To this day, Tretiak can-
not figure out why Plante decided to help him.
"I'm still puzzled by what motivated him to do
that," said Tretiak. "He probably felt sorry for
me, the little guy, in whom Esposito was going
to shoot holes."

The majority of the talk in the Canadian dressing room after the game was how they were
going to solve the Tretiak dilemma. They knew
the 20-year-old was still developing, but he
was still proving to be a problem for Canada's
top scorers. Tretiak was the obvious difference
in the series and frustrated Canada's best for the
entire eight games before Paul Henderson ended
Tretiak's hopes with his famous game—and
series-winning goal.

Up until Henderson's famous goal, the talk of
the entire tournament was on Tretiak and his
constant ability to frustrate Team Canada. After
the Summit Series, the Soviet player kept the

accolades coming his way with more brilliant performances.

"If there is a comparison to an NHL goalie I would make for Tretiak, it would be Terry Sawchuk," said Paul Henderson.

Tretiak was not as adventurous as Sawchuk, but he had his incredible lightning quick reflexes and amazing agility. On more than one occasion, when a Canadian player thought he had Tretiak beat, suddenly a pad or glove would flash across the goal mouth to make the save. He had incredible patience when facing a shooter and always let them make the first move. He never guessed at what the player might do because if he was wrong, the shooter would have an open net. With each level he attained, Tretiak stepped up to every challenge and seemed to get better and better as time went on.

In his time playing with the Soviet national team, Tretiak won three Olympic gold medals, one silver medal, ten world championships and countless other tournaments. There was just one thing left in his career that he had yet to accomplish—a spot on an NHL team.

By 1983, National Hockey League managers were well acquainted with Tretiak's work, but no team was more interested than the Montréal Canadiens, who saw fit to draft him 143rd overall that year. After leading the Soviet team to another gold medal at the 1984 Olympic Games in Sarajevo, Tretiak was sure that the USSR would release him to play in the National Hockey League, but travel restrictions kept him from ever testing himself in the North American market. Deeply angered by his country's refusal to allow him to play, Tretiak announced his retirement from hockey at the age of 32.

Tretiak said, "I was ready to come here for so long, and I think I would have done well. I've dedicated my whole life to hockey, and I would have given playing in the NHL 150%."

Despite never playing a single game for a North American professional team, Tretiak became the first European be inducted into the Hockey Hall of Fame for his contributions to the game of hockey. Tretiak finally did make it into the NHL, as a goaltender coach rather than as a player, when the Chicago Blackhawks hired him on in 1990 to mentor a rookie goalie by the name of Eddie Belfour. Tretiak still runs a hockey school for goaltenders, passing down the wealth of experience he gained over his illustrious career to a new generation.

Ken Dryden

For any fan of the art of goaltending it's impossible to forget the famous contemplative pose that Ken Dryden assumed whenever there was a stoppage in play. Standing tall, he would place his stick under his chin and survey the ice like some noble sage meditating on the task that lay before him.

From the moment he first came into the world of professional hockey, it was clear that Dryden was unlike any other athlete in the game. More interested in getting his law degree than stopping pucks in the NHL, Dryden made sure in his contract negotiations with the Montréal Canadiens that he would have time to pursue his degree while playing for the team. The Canadiens gladly accommodated Dryden's need because the 6'4", 205-pound goaltender was one of the best they had seen in a long time.

The Canadiens line up of the 1970s was not the easiest to crack. With a roster full of veteran and rookie talent, the Canadiens did not just call up any player from the minors. A player had to earn his spot, and it wasn't easy. Dryden impressed enough people on the farm team to get called to play for the Canadiens in the final few games of the 1970–71 season. Dryden won the final six games of the season and only allowed in 9 goals for a goals-against average of 1.65.

On March 20, 1971, Dryden was just a few games into his first stint in the NHL, and he was already making history. That night, Ken Dryden's Montréal Canadiens went up against his older brother Dave's Buffalo Sabres before a Montréal crowd anxious to see the brothers do battle. But the Canadiens started Rogie Vachon that night, and the two brothers were forced to watch from the sidelines. But when Vachon sustained an injury in the second period, the fans got their wish. Dryden was sent out to replace him. Buffalo coach Punch Imlach immediately pulled his goal-tender in favour of the older Dryden. History was made as two brothers faced off against each other in nets for the first time in the National Hockey League. The younger Dryden got the upper hand in the match, with a 5–2 win. After the game was over, the two brothers skated to centre ice and shook hands, much to the delight of the Montréal Forum crowd.

Things just kept getting better for Dryden as the Canadiens headed into the post-season. Rookies don't always get a chance at playing in the playoffs after just six games, but Dryden's performance made it an easy decision to start him rather than regular goaltender Rogie Vachon. Many fans were critical of putting in a rookie goaltender to start the playoffs, especially after Dryden lost the first game of the quarterfinals against the Boston Bruins. Canadiens coach Al MacNeil stuck with his goaltender, and it paid off. With Dryden's clutch goaltending, the Canadiens eliminated the defending champion Boston Bruins in seven games and then took out the Minnesota North Stars in six games. They defeated the Chicago Blackhawks in the Stanley Cup finals in a difficult seven-game series. Although the Canadiens' Frank Mahovlich scored 14 goals and had 27 points to lead the playoff scoring race, a feat worthy of the Conn Smythe Trophy as most valuable player, that distinction went straight to Dryden for his rookie performance.

Some critics were initially surprised at Dryden's success. Goaltenders of his size would normally cover a lot of net, but their agility and speed were often compromised. Dryden was the first big goaltender who had the complete package. He was also a student of the game. By approaching the game with the same attitude as his studies, Dryden was as strong mentally as he was physically. The Canadiens were a much better team for it.

In Kevin Allen's book, *Without Fear*, former teammate Larry Pleau tried to sum up Dryden's impact after his first two seasons with the Canadiens. "There was no description or category that fit Ken Dryden because what he did never happened before. How do you sum up a goalie that wins the Stanley Cup the season before he wins the Calder Trophy as Rookie of the Year?"

Although the Canadiens did not win the Cup the next year, Dryden was honoured as the rookie of the year. He was already the dominant goaltender in the league, able to change the course of a game by the way he played.

By the end of the 1972–73 season, Dryden was at the top of his game. He won his first Vezina Trophy and took home his second Stanley Cup with another brilliant performance in the playoffs. But as suddenly as he arrived on the scene, Dryden acknowledged that his career was probably over during the summer before the start of the 1973–74 season.

Not able to come to an agreement with the Canadiens management on a new contract, Dryden stuck to his principles and sat out the entire 1973–74 season. He spent his time off working in a law office in Toronto as an articling student earning a salary of $7500. Dryden's pressure tactics worked as the Canadiens suffered through a difficult season without their star in nets. During the off-season, the Canadiens came to an agreement with Dryden, and he was back between the pipes for the 1974–75 season.

Dryden was a little rusty in his first season back, but by 1975–76, he was back in full form, and so were the Canadiens. From that season until 1979, Dryden won four more Stanley Cups and four Vezina Trophies, and he never had a goals-against average higher than 2.30.

At the end of his 1979 Cup conquest, Dryden surprised the hockey world and announced that he was leaving hockey to pursue his career in law. It didn't make any sense to those who didn't know him, but to those in his circle it was perfectly reasonable. Hockey was a challenge that he had conquered, and he wanted to move onto other things in his life. Soon after his retirement, he published an excellent book called *The Game*, a cerebral look into his time spent in and around the game of hockey.

Dryden never did leave the game completely. In 1997, he was hired to help rebuild the Toronto Maple Leafs franchise and quickly turned a mediocre team back into one of the best in the league. His most recent achievement was his election to Canada's House of Commons as a Member of Parliament for the Toronto riding of York Centre.

He set his sights even higher in a bid to become the leader of the Liberal Party and maybe even one day the prime minister of Canada. Not bad for a hockey player!

Bernie Parent

"Only the Lord Saves More than Bernie Parent!" read the bumper stickers on Philadelphia Flyers fans' cars. That sort of respect from hockey fans doesn't come easily, and Bernie Parent had to pay his dues before he earned the recognition that he knew he deserved.

Parent, like Glenn Hall, liked to describe hockey as "sixty minutes of hell," but unlike Hall, who was nervous before every game, Parent relished every second of it. Often the joker on a team, Parent made everyone around him feel at ease. But when it came time to play, Parent was all business. He was a pure stand-up goaltender like his hero and mentor Jacques Plante. As a kid growing up in Montréal during the Canadiens greatest days in the 1950s, Parent studied Plante's every move on the ice. The way he played the angles, how he came out to meet the shooters and how he played the puck. Parent even had the same odd demeanour that drove his coaches crazy, just like Plante.

"You don't have to be crazy to be a goalie," Parent said, "but it helps!"

But unlike his hero, success did not come instantly for Parent. As part of the Bruins farm system in 1965, he had a chance in the 1965–66 and 1966–67 seasons to become the Bruins number-one goaltender, but he didn't live up to the expectations of the Bruins coaching staff, registering a goals-against average of over 3.60 for both years. The Bruins felt more confident in the abilities of their other prospect, Gerry Cheevers. When the league expanded in 1967, Parent was left unprotected, and he was picked up by the new Philadelphia Flyers franchise.

Parent played well in his first few years with the Flyers, but the team was not yet the power-house they were to become during the early '70s. Trying to get out of their post-expansion slump, in 1971 the Flyers organized a trade with the Maple Leafs that included Parent. The Flyers relied on another young goaltender named Doug Favell, hoping that he would become the netminder they needed to take them far into the playoffs.

In Toronto, Parent was living a childhood dream, playing on the same team as his hero

Jacques Plante. Parent learned a lot from the veteran netminder during his two brief seasons with the Leafs. The two goalies worked together to improve the finer aspects of their game. Even after Plante retired from the game, he would regularly speak to Parent over the phone or fly from his home in Switzerland to help him with the physical and mental aspects of his game. "Plante was like a god to me," Parent later admitted. "Now I was on the same team with him."

Parent left the Toronto Maple Leafs in 1972 to join the new World Hockey Association. He found that what he learned from Plante improved his game significantly and gave him a renewed confidence that he had never felt before in his professional career. Parent played 63 games for the Philadelphia Blazers, but at the end of the season, the franchise had to fold operations because of financial difficulties. Faced with the prospect of returning to the Leafs, Parent demanded a trade returning him to the Flyers. Philadelphia was more than happy to accommodate Parent after struggling to make it into the playoffs in the years without him on the team. Within the first few games of season, the Flyers knew they could finally make a solid run to the Cup with Parent guarding their nets.

Teammate and backup goaltender Bobby Taylor summed up Parent's brilliance on the ice.

"He was by far the best I ever saw. Bernie played 65 games a year and there would only be a handful of bad performances. The rest weren't just good but great. Technically, he was the soundest of any goalie who ever played the game."

High praise, but during the 1973–74 and 1974–75 seasons, Bernie Parent earned every single word of it. After an incredible regular season in 1973–74, when he posted a 1.89 goals-against average, Parent shared the Vezina Trophy with Chicago's Tony Esposito. He also took his Flyers into the playoffs with confidence that they could overcome the toughest challenges. After disposing of the Atlanta Flames in the opening round, the Flyers managed to get by the New York Rangers in the semifinals in seven close games to move on to the Stanley Cup finals against the mighty Boston Bruins. Although the Bruins had home ice advantage and the firepower of Phil Esposito, Bobby Orr and Ken Hodge, Bernie Parent was more than ready for the task of shutting down the league's most powerful offense. Parent kept the Bruins off the score sheet just enough for his team to take a 3–2 series lead. He shut Boston down completely in game six with a final score of 1–0 to win his first ever Stanley Cup. Without Parent, the Flyers surely would have fallen out of the playoffs much earlier. For his heroic efforts, he received the Conn Smythe Trophy as the most valuable player in the playoffs.

Parent repeated his incredible performance for the 1974–75 regular season. He finished alone atop the leading goaltenders, assuring himself the Vezina Trophy honours and confidence going into another playoff year. Against the Flyers' first round opponents, the Maple Leafs, Parent posted two shutout victories in a four-game sweep of the series. Parent put in a brilliant performance during the semifinals against the New York Islanders, again posting two shutouts, but it took seven games before the Flyers could advance to the finals to face off against the Buffalo Sabers. Although the Sabres put in a valiant effort, Parent was once again the reason for the Flyers' success, shutting the Sabres out in game six to win his second Stanley Cup and another Conn Smythe Trophy as the most valuable player in the play-offs. "We know the exhilarating feeling only a player on a Stanley Cup winner can appreciate," Parent said after winning his second Cup.

Back problems kept Parent out for most of the 1975–76 season, but he returned for the playoffs and led the Flyers again to the finals against the Montréal Canadiens. The Canadiens were just too strong for the Flyers, and they were eliminated in four straight games. Parent recovered from the loss and played three more good seasons, but he could not get his team back into the Stanley Cup finals.

Unfortunately for Parent, his illustrious career ended in a freak accident halfway through the 1978–79 season. During a game, a stick struck him in the right eye, causing permanent damage to his depth perception. At the age of 34, Parent was forced to hang up his skates and take a coaching job with the Flyers as a goaltending advisor. Just like Plante had helped him become a better goaltender, he was now helping other young goalies realize their full potential. Parent was inducted into the Hockey Hall of Fame in 1984.

Billy Smith

Anyone brave enough to stand in front of Billy Smith's net would come away with the bruises to prove it. A fierce competitor, Smith protected the front of his net like it was his own home. If a player got in his way, Smith was never afraid to let him know that he had to move. Most of the time, he tried to do this when the referee wasn't looking, but he was often caught and earned himself a record number of penalty minutes for a goaltender. Smith had a clear justi-fication for his violent ways. "A goaltender has to protect his crease," Smith said. "If they're going to come that close, I have to use any means to get them out of there. If I have to use my stick, I'll use my stick."

Although Smith got his start in the National Hockey League playing just five games with the Los Angeles Kings, Billy Smith spent the rest of his career with the New York Islanders. His com-petitive spirit was needed during the first few years of the expansion team's existence. Billy Smith's competitiveness often brought him into conflict with opposing players, with the media, with his coaches and even with fellow players. But everyone knew that when game time came around, he was the hardest on himself.

After their first few years languishing in the basement of the league, the Islanders finally put together a winning combination for the 1974–75 season, and Smith's goals-against average went from 4.16 in 1972–73 to 2.78 in 1974–75. The Islanders became a good team in the late '70s, but they lacked the experience to go far in the playoffs. But as time went on, the Islanders added players such as Bryan Trottier, Mike Bossy and Clark Gilles who brought the raw talent and experience the team needed to make it anywhere during a time when the Montréal

Canadiens, Boston Bruins and the Philadelphia Flyers dominated the league. The team's patience paid off, and by the end of the 1978–79 regular season, the New York Islanders were the best team in the league. After another early exit from the playoffs at the hands of the New York Rangers, the Islanders started off the new 1979–80 season with a lot of promise.

Smith had a feeling that things were going to go well for the team when he became the first goaltender to be credited with scoring a goal. It was November 28, 1979, and the Islanders were playing the Colorado Rockies in Denver. The play in question came in the third period. The referee signaled a delayed penalty against the Islanders, and the Rockies pulled their goaltender for an extra attacker. The puck was shot into the Islanders zone, touching Smith's chest protector before being picked up by Rockies defenseman Rob Ramage who made a blind pass back to the position he had just left. The puck slowly traveled along the ice and into the Rockies empty net. As the last Islander to touch the puck, Billy Smith got the credit, making him the first goaltender in NHL history to "score" with a goal.

The Islanders finished the 1979–80 season in a respectable fifth place overall but it was in the playoffs that the Islanders and Smith really shone. On their way to the Stanley Cup finals,

Smith helped push aside the Los Angeles Kings, the Boston Bruins and the Buffalo Sabres before meeting the Philadelphia Flyers for the Cup. Along the way, Smith's confidence only grew. He recalled in Chris McDonell's book, *Hockey's Greatest Stars*, "When it came to the playoffs, I always seemed to get on a roll. There was more pressure, which helped my concentration, and the game seemed a little easier."

The Flyers put up a good fight in the finals, but Smith kept them frustrated every game with his aggressive style of play and eventually beat Philadelphia in six games to win his first Stanley Cup. Smith's domination of the playoffs continued for the next three seasons as the Islanders became only the second NHL team to win four Cups in a row. Along the way, Smith won a Vezina Trophy and a Conn Smythe Trophy for his efforts. The Islanders made it again to the finals in 1984, vying for a fifth consecutive Stanley Cup, but they ran into Wayne Gretzky and the Edmonton Oilers who were out for revenge after the Islanders had eliminated them in the finals the previous year.

After their loss in the finals in 1984, wins didn't come as easily for the Islanders with an aging group of veterans and the dominance of other teams like the Edmonton Oilers, Philadelphia Flyers, Calgary Flames and Montréal Canadiens.

By the 1988–89 season, the Islanders once again returned to the bottom of the league. Smith decided it was the right time for him to get out of hockey. He stayed on as a goaltending coach with the Islanders and later with the Florida Panthers. Although he made a lot of enemies during his playing days, Smith was honoured in 1993 when he was inducted into the Hockey Hall of Fame.

Pelle Lindbergh

Long considered one of the greatest net-minders to come out of Sweden, Pelle Lindbergh started his NHL career with the Philadelphia Flyers. The future looked very bright for the young phenom.

The Flyers first noticed Lindbergh playing for Sweden in a game against Czechoslovakia during the 1980 Olympic hockey tournament. The Czechs were by far the better team, constantly on the puck and firing shots on Lindbergh from all angles. The Swedes were out-shot 36 to 16, but Lindbergh's goaltending made the difference in a 4–2 victory for Sweden.

Blessed with lightning-quick reflexes and excellent technical skills, Lindbergh played the game like Grant Fuhr. The Swedish goalie impressed wherever he played. "I've never seen a goalie with such fast legs," said goaltending legend Jacques Plante.

The Philadelphia Flyers also were impressed and signed him to his first professional contract in 1980. After playing for a full season with the Flyers farm team in Portland, Maine, Lindbergh finally realized his dream when he played eight games during the 1981–82 regular NHL season. He impressed the Philadelphia brass enough to earn a spot on the team and played 40 games during the regular season with a respectable 2.98 goals-against average.

Lindbergh's career peaked during the 1984–85 season. He played in 65 games and led the Flyers to the top spot in the league. For his amazing efforts, he received the Vezina Trophy, the highest honour a goaltender can receive and a first for a European player. Lindbergh helped the Flyers into the 1985 playoffs by getting them past their first round opponents, the New York Rangers. Then Philadelphia defeated the New York Islanders with Lindbergh registering two shutouts. The Québec Nordiques fell in six games, but Lindbergh's luck ran out when he met Wayne Gretzky and the Edmonton Oilers, who eliminated the Flyers in five games.

Lindbergh signed a six-year deal with the Flyers during the off-season and immediately went out and bought himself the car of his dreams, a Porsche. Just eight games into the 1985–86 season, Lindbergh hit a concrete wall while driving in New Jersey. Although Lindbergh initially survived the crash, he was left in a vegetative state with little hope of regaining a semblance of normal life. His parents made the difficult decision to disconnect the artificial life support on November 10, 1985, ending his promise of an illustrious career as one of the league's top goaltenders.

Ron Hextall

Often compared to Billy Smith because of his aggressive temperament, Hextall wielded his stick with impunity. Often controversial, always fun to watch, Ron Hextall quickly became one of the greatest goaltenders of his time.

Hextall first came into the league with the Philadelphia Flyers for the 1986–87 season and fast established himself as one of the best goaltenders. The league had never seen a goal-tender who played like Hextall. Jacques Plante was known for wandering from the net to play the puck, but Hextall took it to a new level. Most goaltenders at the time simply left the net to stop the puck for their defensemen and occasionally made short passes with weak backhands. Hextall did things differently. He would use his stick like a defenceman or forward to start a play from his zone, making heads-up passes and even scoring a goal or two once in a while. His teammates even used to pass the puck back to Hextall, who acted almost as a third defenceman. Once his hands dropped into the shooter's position, Hextall could fire outlet passes, bounce the puck off the glass and even lob the puck to avoid an icing call.

His skills helped propel the Philadelphia Flyers into second place overall by the end of the regular season, and Hextall earned himself the Vezina Trophy as the top goaltender in the league. With the regular season having gone so well, the Flyers were one of the most favoured teams to make it to the finals. Hextall put in brilliant performance after brilliant performance as the Flyers dispensed with the New York Rangers, then the Islanders in a nail-biting seven-game series. Next were the defending Stanley Cup champion Montréal Canadiens in six games and the finals against the Edmonton Oilers.

Edmonton won the first two games of the series, but the Flyers came back to tie the series on the strength of Hextall's performance in game six, forcing an exciting game seven final. The Flyers went up early by one goal, but Edmonton came back with three unanswered goals to win the game and the Stanley Cup. Despite the game seven loss, Hextall was named the most valuable player and took home the Conn Smythe Trophy for his efforts.

When Ron Hextall entered the NHL as a rookie, he proudly declared that one day he would score a goal. "I've worked on my shot a lot. I can hit the net from our zone. I've even practiced a bank shot. I'm just waiting for the right situation," said the confident young rookie. Just one year later, he would achieve his dream of becoming the first goaltender to shoot a puck into the opposition's net.

On December 8, 1987, during a game against the Chicago Blackhawks, the Flyers were up by two goals with one minute remaining in the game. The Hawks pulled their goalie in favour of an extra attacker. Then came the mistake Hextall had been waiting for. Hextall got the puck on a bad dump-in by the Hawks, dropped his hands in the shooting position, took one last look at the empty net and fired the puck down the ice into the open net. Scoring one goal wasn't enough for Hextall, who repeated his amazing achievement the following year with another in the playoffs against the Washington Capitals. "I don't mean to sound cocky," Hextall said after scoring his first goal. "But I knew it was just a matter of time before I flipped one in."

Scoring goals was not the only thing Hextall used his stick for. In his rookie year, opposing players quickly became aware of Hextall's aggressive attitude when someone was around his net. In the 1986–87 season, Hextall had amassed a record number of penalty minutes for a goaltender with 104 minutes served. During the Stanley Cup final series against the Edmonton Oilers in 1987, he viciously slashed the Oilers' Kent Nilsson and was suspended for eight games the following season. In the 1989 playoffs, when the Montréal Canadiens were about to eliminate the Philadelphia Flyers, Hextall charged Canadiens defenceman Chris Chelios and attacked him, repeatedly hitting him with his blocker and glove.

After spending one season each with the Québec Nordiques and the New York Islanders, Hextall was back with the Philadelphia Flyers by 1995 and in 1997 helped them back into the Stanley Cup finals against the Detroit Red Wings. But that was as close as Hextall would get to the Stanley Cup. The Red Wings won the series in four games and Hextall never made it back to the finals.

He retired from active duty in 1999, but he has recently made his return to hockey. In June of 2006, Ron Hextall was named the Los Angeles Kings' assistant general manager and general manager of their farm team, the Manchester Monarchs of the American Hockey League.

Patrick Roy

Coming into the National Hockey League being drafted 51st overall in 1984 and with a goals-against average of 5.55 in his final year with the Granby Bisons of the Québec Major Junior Hockey League did not offer much hope for a young goaltender trying to make it on to one of the most storied franchises in hockey history. But the Montréal Canadiens management saw a competitive spirit in the young Patrick Roy that they hoped would propel him to the top. They had no idea how far Roy would push himself.

At the Montréal training camp, Roy met goaltending coach Francois Allaire, who trained the rookie to use the butterfly style. Allaire noticed that Roy was having some problems with goals in the lower part of the net, but by the time Roy got to play in his first game, he had perfected the butterfly and found himself a regular spot on the team.

Roy got his chance to prove himself during the 1985–86 season, playing in 47 regular-season games and posting a 3.35 goals-against average, a respectable number during the high-scoring 1980s. But it was in the playoffs that Roy made a name for himself.

After defeating Boston in an easy best-of-five series, Roy proved himself to be a true clutch goaltender during the division finals against the Hartford Whalers. With a team of rookies, there was little hope that Montréal would make it into the finals, but with each game, Roy's confidence grew, which in turn helped his teammates. The Hartford series was Roy's toughest challenge as the Whalers pounded the Montréal net with shot after shot, but Roy kept every game close, helping his team into the seventh and deciding game. They needed overtime to do it, but with Roy's stellar performance, the Canadiens managed to get the series-winning goal and advance further into the playoffs.

During their next series against the Rangers, Roy was the reason for the Canadiens' win in five games. By then, the Montréal Forum crowd, notorious for demanding instant success from new players, immediately got behind Roy. "The tension was overwhelming, and the fans were screaming 'Rooouuu-ah, Rooouuu-ah.' It got me off to a good start in the NHL," said Roy of one of his most memorable moments in hockey.

Next came the Calgary Flames' turn to try and break the rookie goaltender in the finals, but Roy put up a brick wall in front of the Montréal goal and helped the Canadiens win their 23rd Stanley Cup in five games. Roy finished the playoffs with a 1.92 goals-against average and his first Conn Smythe Trophy as the most valuable player. The young goalie had the essential ingredient that all coaches seek—he could perform under pressure. "The more pressure there is, the more I like it," said Roy about his Stanley Cup, and Conn Smythe Trophy, winning performance.

Roy was an excellent athlete with quick reflexes, but his true talent came from his mental game. Apart from being the best goaltender under pressure, Roy had a unique ability to see the ice and where the shots would come in almost before they were taken. He knew every shooter's habits, read every possible hockey report, and had a confidence that sometimes bordered on cockiness.

Through the 1980s, Patrick Roy, along with Brian Hayward, kept the Canadiens near the top of the league standings, taking home several William Jennings Trophies (awarded to the goaltender with the fewest goals against) and his first Vezina Trophy in 1989. He led the Canadiens back to the finals in 1989 against the Calgary Flames, but this time, the Flames had the upper hand and won the Cup in six games.

Roy won another two Vezina Trophies in 1990 and 1992 and led the Canadiens back into the playoffs in 1993 on the strength of his performances. As the Canadiens made their way through several difficult series, Roy once again found all the pressure on his shoulders to lead a team of rookies into the Stanley Cup finals. Making it past the New York Islanders in the conference finals, the Canadiens faced off against Wayne Gretzky and the Los Angeles Kings. After a tough 4–1 loss in the opener, Roy secured his title as one of the greatest pressure goaltenders of all time, helping the Canadiens win the next three games in overtime. He was so sure of himself that he even had the nerve to wink at Kings forward Tomas Sandstrom after stopping him on a break-away in game four overtime. The Canadiens ended up winning the series and the Stanley Cup in five games. Roy brought home another Conn Smythe Trophy for his heroic efforts.

His fortunes with the Canadiens, however, were about to run out. After the team failed to make the playoffs in 1995, the hard-to-please Montréal media put the blame squarely on Roy's shoulders. When management hired former Canadiens player Mario Tremblay as head coach and Rejean Houle as general manager, Roy's days in Montréal were numbered.

In the Montréal press, rumors quickly began to circulate that Roy and Tremblay did not get along. The feud became public knowledge when the Detroit Red Wings rolled into town on December 2, 1995. After Roy let in several easy goals, the fans at the Forum started to cheer sarcastically every time he made a save. It was clear that Roy was not having a good night, but still Tremblay refused to pull his number-one goaltender. After the goalie let in his ninth goal, Tremblay finally pulled Roy out. For Roy, this was the last straw in an already strained relationship with the Canadiens coach and upper management. Leaving the ice, Roy removed his helmet, walked past Tremblay, turned around immediately, walked over to team president Ronald Corey, and told him he had just played his last game for the Montréal Canadiens. A few days later, he was traded to the Colorado Avalanche, where he found new life and continued to be among the top goaltenders in the league.

That same year with the Avalanche, Roy led his team to second place overall at the end of the regular season and all the way through the play-offs to the Stanley Cup. Roy kept the Colorado Avalanche near the top of the league for several seasons and led them back into the Stanley Cup finals in 2001 against the New Jersey Devils. The goalie made all the difference in the Avalanche's run to the Stanley Cup in a thrilling seven-game series. Roy was named the most valuable player for the third time in his career.

After 18 seasons in the National Hockey League, Patrick Roy announced that he was retiring from the game. Although he probably still had a few good years left in him, Roy felt he had accomplished what he needed and wanted to move onto new challenges. Winning a record 551 games and becoming the only player to have ever won three Conn Smythe Trophies, maybe he had accomplished everything. And on November 13, 2006, Patrick Roy was inducted into the Hockey Hall of Fame as arguably the greatest goaltender to play the game.

The secret of his success? "A goalie has to show he's confident, to his teammates as well as himself. You are the last guy before that special red line. You make yourself confident. You make yourself hard to beat," explained Roy.

Dominic Hasek

He is impossible to classify, his style is unorthodox, and yet he seems to stop anything that comes his way. His one-time Buffalo Sabres coach Ted Nolan tried to classify how his former goaltender plays the game, "Totally, and I mean totally, unpredictable."

It was exactly this unpredictable, unclassifiable style that kept him from appearing in the league after the Chicago Blackhawks drafted him 207th overall in 1983. Hasek had little interest in going to North America to play for the Hawks and played for several years on Czechoslovakian club teams and the national team. He finally joined the Chicago organization, but the Hawks did not like his unconventional style and had already invested more in rookie Eddie Belfour. They traded him to the Buffalo Sabres in 1992.

Just one season later, Hasek, now dubbed the Dominator, led the league with a 1.95 goals-against average (the first below 2.00 since Bernie Parent had 1.89 in 1974) and took home the Vezina and William Jennings trophies for his efforts.

For those that did not believe in Hasek early in his career, his success in Buffalo was sweet revenge. But barely anyone could figure out how he did it. Every time a shot would come in, he would almost certainly flop to his knees, bending and twisting his body in every direction to make a save. One of his greatest assets was his patience. He would wait out shooters until the last second, and they had no idea how he was going to react, giving Hasek the upper hand on most shots.

The strange style worked in Hasek's favour, and he won five Vezina Trophies by the time the 1999 playoffs rolled around. Despite his amazing record until then, he had yet to find any luck in the playoffs. At last, Hasek made his first appearance in the 1999 finals but lost in a heartbreaker to the Dallas Stars in game six overtime.

Apart from the accolades, things were not going well for Hasek off the ice in Buffalo after several well-publicized blowups with the coaching staff and the media. It seemed only a matter of time before Hasek found himself in a new town. In 2001–02, the Detroit Red Wings signed him to a short-term contract. Buffalo could no longer handle the controversy or Hasek's large salary. It was a move that would change his career.

With Buffalo, Hasek had been able to make a good team great, but with Detroit, Hasek changed a great team into a legendary one. Detroit finished the regular season at the top of the standings and sat in a comfortable spot headed into the playoffs. Hasek played excellent hockey through 23 games in the playoffs, frustrating every shooter with his unconventional saves at key moments. Apart from the series against the Colorado Avalanche that went to seven games, the Red Wings coasted through to the finals and dispensed with the Carolina Hurricanes in five games. Hasek finally had his first Stanley Cup victory at the age of 37.

After two more seasons with Detroit, sitting out most of the season with a groin injury, his contract ran out. Hasek signed with another Stanley Cup contender, the Ottawa Senators, for the 2005–06 season. At the age of 41, Hasek was having a career year by the halfway point in the season. But he injured his groin again and was forced to sit out the last half of the season. There is no doubt he can still play in the NHL and be effective for another few years. But the question remains: can he stay healthy? Whenever he does retire, there will no doubt be a spot waiting for him in the Hockey Hall of Fame.

Ed Belfour

It's a pretty good sign if in your rookie year as a goaltender in the NHL, you win the Vezina Trophy and the Calder Trophy. That is what the Chicago Blackhawks hoped would happen when they started 25-year-old Ed Belfour for the 1990–91 regular season. He had already played a few games for them in previous seasons, and they liked what they saw enough to start him in 74 regular season games. Belfour helped Chicago finish first in the league for the first time since the 1969–70 season, when Tony Esposito, another Vezina-and Calder-winning goaltender, led the team.

Belfour proved himself in his second year, taking the Blackhawks into the 1992 Stanley Cup finals for the first time since 1973. The Pittsburgh Penguins repeated as champions, but Belfour had established himself as one of the premier goaltenders in the league in just two short years.

Belfour continued to play well through the 1990s, winning 304 games, coming just second behind Patrick Roy at 317. However, Chicago's early exits from the playoffs left a stigma attached to Belfour that he wasn't able to handle the pressure. He was criticized for his tendency to guess too early where a player would shoot the puck and a butterfly style that covered the bottom half of the net but often left him open for high glove-hand shots. Although he played well, the Chicago Blackhawks wanted a change in goal and traded him to the San Jose Sharks. The critics were proven correct as Belfour's goals-against average jumped to a career high of 3.41. He played just 13 games with San Jose before signing as a free agent in 1997 with the resurgent Dallas Stars.

Belfour finally got the respect he deserved in the league and silenced all the critics who said he would never win a championship when he led the Stars to the Stanley Cup. The goalie posted a low 1.67 goals-against average and had three shutouts.

Former NHL player Peter McNab characterized Belfour in Allen's book, *Without Fear*. "He epitomizes the term battler. You can't define his style. As unorthodox as Dominik Hasek is and as much of a technician as Patrick Roy is, all you can say about Belfour is that he is a battler. When he won that Cup, that justified saying he is great."

But Belfour was getting older, and the Dallas Stars wanted to build their team around rookie goaltending sensation Marty Turco. By 2001–02, the direction that the Stars wanted to go in was more than apparent to Belfour. In July 2002, Belfour signed with the Toronto Maple Leafs. In his three years with the Leafs, Belfour finally passed Terry Sawchuk on the all-time-wins list at 447, but during the 2005–06 season, he was bothered by injuries and his goals-against average jumped to a dismal 3.45. The Leafs released him to the free agent market during the off-season. On July 25, 2006, he signed with the Florida Panthers at the age of 41.

Martin Brodeur

One of the best all-around goaltenders in hockey history, Martin Brodeur is nowhere near finished, and he has already attained the level of living legend.

In an era where almost every goaltender has switched to the butterfly style, Martin Brodeur plays in the old-fashioned stand-up style, just modified to fit the modern game. He has the athleticism of Jacques Plante, the glove hand of Patrick Roy and the stickhandling abilities of Ron Hextall. But his greatest attribute has to be his ability to remain completely calm under the heaviest pressure.

"I don't get too concerned about the game," said Brodeur in Kevin Allen's book, *Without Fear*. "I go out there and really enjoy myself. I don't make it hard on myself. I don't put extra pressure on myself. When you are full of confidence, I think it helps you play a lot of games. You don't feel the pressure. That's when a goalie gets tired—when they feel the pressure."

Martin Brodeur's introduction to goaltending came at an early age. His father, Dennis, was the goaltender for Canada's bronze-medal-winning

Olympic hockey team at the 1956 Olympics in Cortina, Italy. More importantly, young Brodeur's father was the official photographer for the Montréal Canadiens, and Martin had the privilege of going to many of the games and practices. The boy would sit in the old Montréal Forum and dream about one day playing for the Canadiens and being a goaltender like his idol Patrick Roy.

"He was a young guy from Montréal, like me,"said Brodeur speaking of his boyhood days in Montréal. "I idolized him because he came in to the NHL so young and he showed he could do the job. He made me see the possibility of doing it myself." After getting drafted 20th overall by the New Jersey Devils in 1990, Brodeur was finally called up from the minors and became New Jersey's number-one goaltender for the 1993–94 season. Brodeur was genuinely nervous in his debut game against the Boston Bruins, but after stopping the first shot, he went on to lead the Devils to a 4–2 victory. Since joining the league New Jersey had never really been a serious contender during the regular season or the few times that they made the playoffs, only getting as far as the conference finals in 1988. Brodeur brought an element of reliability to the team and a confidence that they had the goaltending to go far into the playoffs. The Devils went from finishing the 1992–93 regular season with 87 points to earning 106 points by the end of the 1993–94 season thanks to the efforts of their rookie goaltender. The Calder Trophy–winning goaltender took his team all the way to the conference finals only to be defeated by the eventual Stanley Cup champion New York Rangers in a thrilling seven-game series that went into double overtime. It was a bitter pill for the rookie goaltender to swallow. He wanted to win the Cup in his rookie year like his boyhood idol Patrick Roy. But he would soon have another chance at glory.

After a shortened 48-game season because of a labour dispute between the NHL Players Association and the league, Brodeur got his chance for revenge in the playoffs. Brodeur recorded three shutouts during the first series against the Boston Bruins, did not allow more than three goals in any one game in the series against the Pittsburgh Penguins and was outstanding in the conference finals against the Philadelphia Flyers. The Devils moved into the Stanley Cup finals for the first time in the franchise's history. Their opponents, the Detroit Red Wings, were not going to be easy to beat with a solid mix of young players and veteran talent. It looked like Brodeur was going to have a tough job keeping the Red Wings off the score sheet, but he was sensational in the series, not allowing more than two goals in one game. The Devils swept their way to the Stanley Cup. Brodeur had his first Cup and a spot alongside the league's top goalies, including his boyhood hero, Patrick Roy.

Despite the Stanley Cup and all the praise he was getting around the league, Martin Brodeur still had not accomplished something that he had set his heart on from the moment he entered the league. "I need a goal now," said Brodeur in 1995. "I'm looking for the chance all the time. If I get it and it doesn't jeopardize my team, I'm going for it." His dreams finally came true during a playoff game against the Montréal Canadiens on April 17, 1997.

Montréal was down two goals late in the third period and pulled goaltender Jocelyn Thibault in favour of an extra attacker. Brodeur, seeing his opportunity, grabbed the puck when it was shot in on a line change and fired it the length of the ice into the empty net. Brodeur now joined Ron Hextall in the small group of goaltenders to have scored a goal.

Things continued at a steady pace for Brodeur. He played regularly in 70 games for the Devils and kept the team near the top of the league each year. By the 2000 playoffs, the New Jersey Devils were one of the premiere teams in the league. Their strong defense and the always-reliable goaltending of Martin Brodeur made New Jersey one of the toughest teams to play against. Once again, Brodeur made it through each round of the playoffs and help beat the Dallas Stars in the finals for his second Stanley Cup. He was back in the finals the following year against the Colorado Avalanche, playing against his hero, Patrick Roy. The mentor still had a few things left to teach his admirer as Roy's Avalanche beat Brodeur's Devils in seven games.

Brodeur added another distinction to his already-illustrious record when he backstopped the Canadian Olympic team to their first gold medal in 50 years at the Salt Lake City Olympics in 2002. Supporting the Canadian team with stellar saves through the rounds, Brodeur held the fort in the gold-medal game against the United States and was one of the major reasons why Canada could call itself the best team in hockey once again.

As if winning an Olympic gold medal for his country wasn't enough, Brodeur returned to the NHL to take his club back into the Stanley Cup finals in 2003 and defeat the Anaheim Mighty Ducks to win his third Stanley Cup and his first Vezina Trophy.

"A lot of people take Ken Dryden for granted by saying he played on great teams," said Brodeur's former coach, Larry Robinson, comparing him to the Canadiens Ken Dryden. "The last time I looked, the goaltender was part of the team. And the reason they were great teams was because they had great goaltending. And Marty gives the Devils great goaltending night in and night out. It's the wins that count." And for Brodeur, the wins will no doubt keep coming.

Chapter Four

PLAYOFF HEROES

Mike Vernon

Always reliable during the regular season, Mike Vernon seemed to come alive during the playoffs. His regular season goals-against average always hovered around the 3.00 mark, and he was never really a factor in backstopping a team to the top of the league standings. But in his rookie season with the Calgary Flames, Vernon came to life in the pressure-filled atmosphere of the Stanley Cup playoffs.

Although he lost in the 1986 finals to the Montréal Canadiens, Vernon was one of the main reasons the Calgary Flames made it that far past some tough opponents. But the 1989 Calgary Flames were much different from the team a few years earlier, and Vernon now stood among the elite goaltenders of the league. The Calgary goalie got his revenge against the Montréal Canadiens in the finals, leading the Flames to their first Stanley Cup in franchise history.

Al MacInnis won the Conn Smythe Trophy, but Vernon's three shutouts and his 2.26 goals-against average made the difference in the playoffs. The Flames remained one of the top teams in the league but could not repeat their amazing 1989 performance. Vernon was traded to the Detroit Red Wings, who had been looking for a solid goaltender to lead them into the playoffs.

Vernon's impact with the Wings was immediate. He led them through the playoff rounds with brilliant performances against Dallas and Chicago on the way to the Stanley Cup finals, a place where Vernon was becoming quite comfortable. Detroit lost to the New Jersey Devils, but they were back for more in the 1997 playoffs. Chris Osgood was the goaltender of choice for the Red Wings during the regular season, but head coach Scotty Bowman decided to play his veteran during the playoffs. Vernon did not disappoint, playing excellent hockey to beat the St. Louis Blues, the Anaheim Mighty Ducks and the Colorado Avalanche to make it into the finals. He even put aside his goaltending duties in the series against the Avalanche and fought Patrick Roy after a brawl broke out. Vernon rode the wave of energy from the Colorado series and used it to sweep the Philadelphia Flyers for his second Stanley Cup. He was recognized as the difference maker in the playoffs and took home the Conn Smythe Trophy as the playoffs' most valuable player.

After spending a few years jumping around the league with the San Jose Sharks and the Florida Panthers, Vernon ended his career where he started, back in Calgary, to be remembered as one of the best playoff goaltenders ever.

Johnny Bower

Like Lorne Worsley, Johnny Bower did not catch a break in the National Hockey League until he was much older. He played a full season with the New York Rangers in 1953–54, but he was sent down to the minors when the team decided to go with Worsley instead. Bower did not get a break until Punch Imlach came on board with the Maple Leafs at which point he finally got his first fulltime assignment at the age of 34.

Under Imlach's guidance, Bower transformed himself into one of the league's top goalies whose fearless style of play helped the Leafs back to the top of the league after playing second fiddle to the Montréal Canadiens and the Detroit Red Wings for a decade. In a few short years, Bower secured the first of his two Vezina Trophies and put the Leafs back in the hunt for their first Stanley Cup since Bill Barilko won it with his overtime goal in 1951.

Bower did more than bring respect back to the Leafs organization. He helped the team to their first Stanley Cup in 10 years, beating the defending champion Chicago Blackhawks in 1962. Bower was the difference for the Leafs again in 1963, using his devastating poke check and fearless attitude to get himself in front of every shot possible in order to win.

"I always played best under pressure," said Bower. "Maybe it was the money and the prestige that went with big games." Either way, Bower was the king of the Leafs through the '60s. He won the Leafs an unprecedented third Stanley Cup in 1964 in a nail-biter of a series against the Detroit Red Wings that went to game seven. Bower, as always, played his best under pressure, shutting out the Wings in the final game to win his third consecutive Stanley Cup. If the Conn Smythe Trophy had been awarded prior to 1965, Bower would have surely earned himself one or two during the Leafs dynasty of the early '60s.

The Montréal Canadiens won the Cup over the next two years, but Bower was not yet finished surprising his detractors. For the 1967 finals against the Canadiens, many people had written off Bower and his goaltending partner Terry Sawchuk as too old to still be playing at such a high level. At 42, Bower was certainly over the hill, but he made all the difference as the Leafs came back from an early loss to Montréal to tie the series and eventually defeat the powerful Canadiens to win the Leafs' last Stanley Cup to date.

"Bower is the most remarkable hockey player I've ever seen," said coach Punch Imlach. "I keep telling him: 'I don't care how old you are. As long as you can stop the puck, you have a job.'"

Stopping the puck was getting to be a little difficult for Bower after the 1967 Cup. He retired just three seasons later as the oldest goaltender ever to play in the NHL at the age of 46.

Grant Fuhr

As a part of the highest-scoring team in the history of the National Hockey League, you might expect a goalie to have an easy job in nets. But that open firewagon style of hockey often left the goaltender to fend for himself on numerous odd-man rushes. The Edmonton Oilers were lucky enough to have Grant Fuhr guarding the nets for them during their 1980s dynasty.

Fuhr was a good goaltender during the regular season, but in the playoffs, he truly came to life. His lightning-fast reflexes often made the difference in close games, and on more than one occasion, his clutch play saved the team. Fuhr was the reason why the Oilers could play the wide-open hockey that characterized the team in the 1980s. With confidence in the goaltender behind them to get the job done, the Oilers were able to rewrite the history books. Fuhr's goal-tending got so good at one point that he could change the course of a game with one single save.

Countless times, Oiler opponents thought they had an open net only to have one of Fuhr's pads or his glove flash across the goal mouth to make the save. His highlight reels look more like miracles than saves made by a mere mortal.

Fuhr's best season came in 1987–88, when he racked up 40 wins in 75 games and gave one of the best playoff performances of his career. Even though he finished the regular season with an goals-against average of 3.43, he still won the Vezina Trophy for his efforts and was just beat out by teammate Wayne Gretzky for the Hart Trophy as the league's most valuable player.

Fuhr was suspended by the Oilers in 1990 after he admitted that he had used cocaine earlier in his career. He came back to help the Oilers to the conference finals in 1991 only to lose to the Minnesota North Stars. Then the team began to sell off all the players that helped build the dynasty of the '80s. Fuhr found himself with the Toronto Maple Leafs. But his time with the Leafs was limited, given that they wanted to invest more into their young rookie Felix Potvin. After two seasons, Fuhr moved to Buffalo where another young goaltender by the name of Dominik Hasek was stealing the show. Again, after a few short seasons, Fuhr was on the move, this time to Los Angeles, where he rejoined former teammate Wayne Gretzky. He lasted only 14 games in L.A. before finding a home with the St. Louis Blues.

Far from being a washed-up goaltender, Fuhr played in a record 79 games, appearing in 76 consecutively, during the 1995–96 season. St. Louis hoped that Fuhr would lead the Blues through the playoffs, but Maple Leafs forward Nick Kypreos ran into Fuhr while he had the puck covered in his crease. Fuhr tore several ligaments in his leg and could not play out the rest of the

Blues playoff run. The Detroit Red Wings later eliminated the Blues.

After another promising season, Fuhr's injuries began to catch up to the aging netminder. Fuhr was traded to the Calgary Flames for the 1999–2000 season after the Blues picked up goaltender Roman Turek from the Dallas Stars. In Calgary, Fuhr played in only 23 regular season games and ended with a 3.83 goals-against average. During that season, Fuhr became only the ninth goaltender in NHL history to win 400 career games, joining the likes of Terry Sawchuk, Jacques Plante, Tony Esposito, Glenn Hall, Ed Belfour, Curtis Joseph, Martin Brodeur and Patrick Roy. But his reflexes were not as fast as they used to be, so during the off-season, Fuhr announced his retirement from hockey.

Lorne "Gump" Worsley

Beginning an NHL career at the age of 24 is considered late for a goaltender, but Worsley never had things easy when it came to hockey. It wasn't until the age of 36 that he finally won his first playoff series with the Montréal Canadiens. Throughout the 1950s, he was the goaltender for the mediocre New York Rangers, who never could get past the stronger teams of that time. Worsley was a good goaltender, but the Rangers needed a change. They were not having any success with their current lineup of players and needed to wipe the slate clean. Worsley wasn't offended, and when he found out he had been traded to Montréal, he was more than happy to make the move. Montréal was his hometown: he had grown up on the streets of the working class district of Point St.Charles and played junior hockey in Verdun. The trade to the Canadiens was like coming home for him.

In Montréal, Worsley seemed to spring to life. He was brought on board to help goalie Charlie Hodge shoulder the load, but he ended up taking the spotlight, leading the Canadiens to the Stanley Cup in 1965, 1966, 1968 and 1969. After tasting champagne from his first Stanley Cup, Worsley smiled from ear to ear. "Nothing has ever matched that thrill!" he said. During that time, he also shared the Vezina Trophy with Charlie Hodge and was a huge oversight for the Conn Smythe Trophy when the Canadiens beat the Detroit Red Wings in the 1966 Stanley Cup final in six games. The trophy went to losing goaltender Roger Crozier.

Worsley won his last Cup with the Canadiens in 1969 and soon found there was no more room for him in the Canadiens lineup because of an ongoing feud with head coach Claude Ruel. After pondering retirement, Worsley was talked into playing a few more years with the Minnesota North Stars, but things did not go well for him with the expansion club, and he lost more games than he won. Plus a more modern problem was starting to wear down his nerves. The normally calm goaltender who never wore a mask up until his final days in the league could not take the constant flying between cities that the new expanded league demanded and decided to hang up his pads after the 1973–74 season at the age of 45.

Chapter Five

GOALTENDING FACT CHECK

Career Regular Season Records

Most Games Played: 1029, Patrick Roy

From the moment he entered the National Hockey League, Patrick Roy regularly played over 50 games per season and rarely relinquished his position because of injury.

Most Minutes Played: 60,233, Patrick Roy

Naturally, by playing in over a thousand games, Roy was bound to win this title. But it also helps that he was hardly ever pulled out of a game as well.

Most Wins: 551, Patrick Roy

Those 551 wins certainly help when deciding who is the greatest goaltender of all time.

Most Losses: 353, Lorne "Gump" Worsley

The record for most career losses speaks more to the longevity of Worsley's career rather than to his skill level. Playing until the age of 45, a goaltender is bound to pick up a few losses along the way.

Most Ties: 172, Terry Sawchuk

It is fitting that the king of shutouts holds the record for the most career ties. A clutch goaltender until the end, Sawchuk could always be relied on to close the door to the opponent whenever his team needed him, even if it meant a tie.

Most Goals Allowed: 2756, Grant Fuhr and Gilles Meloche

Gilles Meloche played his entire 18-year career with mediocre expansion teams, so it is understandable that he allowed a few more goals than most goaltenders. But many fans are shocked that Grant Fuhr, certain future Hall of Fame inductee, finds himself with this dubious distinction attached to his illustrious career. But as a part of the high-scoring Edmonto Oilers of the 1980s, who played pure offensive hockey, Fuhr was often left to his own devices. He might have let in five goals in a game, but he could rely on his team to score seven.

Lowest Goals-against Average: 1.60, Hal Winkler

When you play in just 75 regular season games, it's easier to keep your career goals-against average so low.

Highest Save Percentage: .924, Dominik Hasek

The "Dominator" is one of the most reliable goaltenders around with a consistently high save percentage. With a career that is still going, who knows how high he can go?

Most Shots Faced: 28,353, Patrick Roy

Eighteen years. An incredible 28,353 hard frozen rubber pucks shot at you. It's clear why successful goaltenders are of a different breed.

Most Shutouts: 103, Terry Sawchuk

Recording this many shutouts during an era when natural goal-scorers like Maurice Richard, Bobby Hull, Jean Beliveau, Stan Mikita and Dickie Moore were at their peak was not an easy task. His 103 shutouts prove that Sawchuk was one of the greatest of all time.

Most Points: 48, Tom Barrasso

Goaltenders do not usually get credit for their play-making abilities, but Tom Barrasso loved to play the puck. Passing to players like Mario Lemieux and Jaromir Jagr who can rush from one end of the rink to the other and score, a goaltender is bound to pick up a few assists.

Most Penalty Minutes: 584, Ron Hextall

This one is no surprise. The goaltender who wielded his goal stick like an axe and who never shied away from a fight picked up his fair share of penalties along the way.

Single Season Records

Most Games Played: 79, Grant Fuhr (St. Louis), 1995–96

When many people dismissed Grant Fuhr as a washed-up goaltender, he proved to the hockey world that he still could play like he did in his prime with the Edmonton Oilers.

Most Minutes Played: 4554, Martin Brodeur (New Jersey), 2003–04

Regularly playing in an average of 70 games a season. Martin Brodeur will surely challenge Patrick Roy for the career record.

Most Wins: 47, Bernard Parent (Philadelphia), 1973–74

In 1973–74, Bernie Parent made a name for himself as one of the greatest goaltenders of all time when he won the Vezina Trophy, the Stanley Cup, and the Conn Smythe Trophy.

Most Losses: 48, Gary Smith (California Golden Seals) 1970–1971

Smith had the unfortunate job of minding the goal for one of the worst teams in NHL history.

In 1970–71, he only won 19 games and had a goals-against average of 3.86.

Most Ties: 22, Harry Lumley (Toronto), 1954–55

He would rather have the tie games in the win column, but it beats losing the games.

Most Goals Allowed: 310, Ken McAuley (New York Rangers), 1943–44

It is not surprising to find out that the Rangers won only six games that year and McAuley had a goals-against average of 6.24.

Lowest Goals-against Average: 0.92, George Hainsworth (Montréal), 1928–29

During a season where forward passing was not allowed and defense was the name of the game, Georges Hainsworth worked his way to the best goaltending record in NHL history.

Highest Save Percentage: .937, Dominik Hasek (Buffalo), 1998–99

Hasek's best save-percentage season helped the Buffalo Sabres make it all the way to the Stanley Cup finals that year.

Most Shots Faced: 2488, Roberto Luongo (Florida), 2005–06

Poor, poor Roberto Luongo. Year after year, the Florida Panthers allowed their opponents an average of 40 shots per game. It is a testament to

Luongo's nerve that he kept the team competitive and not an easy team to beat. He will hopefully find some relief in the 2006–07 season with his new team, the Vancouver Canucks.

Most Shutouts: 22, George Hainsworth (Montréal), 1928–29

No one will likely ever come close to this record.

Most Points: 14, Grant Fuhr (Edmonton), 1983–84

Playing with Wayne Gretzky, Mark Messier, Esa Tikkanen, Glen Anderson and many more, the goaltender was likely to pick up a few assists during the season on some of the Oilers' patented end-to-end rushes.

Most Penalty Minutes: 113, Ron Hextall (Philadelphia), 1988–89

Maybe if he had to sit in the penalty box, he would have learned his lesson.

Career Playoff Records

Most Games Played: 247, Patrick Roy

Making appearances in the playoffs in every year in the league except one (1995), Patrick Roy took both the Canadiens and the Avalanche far into the post-season each time.

Most Minutes Played: 15,208, Patrick Roy

Most games played = Most minutes.

Most Wins: 151, Patrick Roy

His 151 wins solidify his place as one of the greatest clutch playoff goaltenders.

Most Losses: 94, Patrick Roy

When you play in 247 playoff games, you are bound to lose a few. Roy's 151 wins to 94 losses is not a bad ratio.

Most Goals Allowed: 584, Patrick Roy

That 584 is a reflection of the number of games Roy played in the playoffs, not a reflection of how good he was.

Lowest Goals-against average: 1.19, Alec Connell

The Ottawa Senators and Montréal Maroons goaltender could always be counted on in the playoffs to keep the game close and the score extremely low.

Most Shutouts: 23, Patrick Roy

Roy is not likely to hold this record for long with Martin Brodeur hot on his heels with 21 career shutouts.

Most Points: 12, Grant Fuhr

The Wayne Gretzky effect! It even gets the goaltender some points.

Most Penalty Minutes: 115, Ron Hextall

Hextall did not help his hunt for a Stanley Cup at all by giving his opponents so many powerplay chances. Probably one of the reasons why he finished his career without a Cup to his name.

Single Season Playoff Records

Most Games Played: 26, Ron Hextall (Philadelphia), 1986–87 and Miikka Kiprusoff (Calgary), 2003–04

Despite both goalies taking their teams all the way to the Stanley Cup finals, their efforts were not rewarded with a championship. Hextall lost to the Edmonton Oilers and Kiprusoff lost to the Tampa Bay Lightning.

Most Minutes Played: 1655, Miikka Kiprusoff (Calgary), 2003–04

He played every minute of every game. Several series even went all the way to game seven, including the Stanley Cup final.

Most Losses: 11, Ron Hextall (Philadelphia), 1986–87 and Miikka Kiprusoff (Calgary), 2003–04

When almost every series goes to seven games and you make it to the Stanley Cup final, you accumulate a few losses.

Most Goals Allowed: 74, Kelly Hrudey (Los Angeles), 1992–93

Despite the many goals allowed, he still managed to backstop the L.A. Kings all the way to the Stanley Cup finals only to lose to the goaltender with the most wins—Patrick Roy and the Montréal Canadiens.

Lowest Goals-against average: 0.60, Alec Connell (Ottawa), 1926–27

During his run to the Stanley Cup championship with the Ottawa Senators, Connell did not let in more than one goal per game.

Most Shutouts: 7, Martin Brodeur (New Jersey), 2002–03

Leading his team with seven shutouts in the post-season, it is no surprise that Martin Brodeur won the Stanley Cup and the Conn Smythe Trophy.

Most Penalty Minutes: 43, Ron Hextall (Philadelphia), 1986–87

Not a good stat to have in your rookie year. Lucky for him, he played well enough to warrant keeping him around.

Vezina Trophy Winners

Year	Player	Team
2006	Miikka Kiprusoff	Calgary Flames
2005	No winner due to the 2004–05 NHL lockout	
2004	Martin Brodeur	New Jersey Devils
2003	Martin Brodeur	New Jersey Devils
2002	Jose Theodore	Montréal Canadiens
2001	Dominik Hasek	Buffalo Sabres
2000	Olaf Kolzig	Washington Capitals
1999	Dominik Hasek	Buffalo Sabres
1998	Dominik Hasek	Buffalo Sabres
1997	Dominik Hasek	Buffalo Sabres
1996	Jim Carey	Washington Capitals
1995	Dominik Hasek	Buffalo Sabres
1994	Dominik Hasek	Buffalo Sabres
1993	Ed Belfour	Chicago Blackhawks
1992	Patrick Roy	Montréal Canadiens
1991	Ed Belfour	Chicago Blackhawks
1990	Patrick Roy	Montréal Canadiens
1989	Patrick Roy	Montréal Canadiens
1988	Grant Fuhr	Edmonton Oilers
1987	Ron Hextall	Philadelphia Flyers
1986	John Vanbiesbrouck	New York Rangers
1985	Pelle Lindbergh	Philadelphia Flyers
1984	Tom Barrasso	Buffalo Sabres
1983	Pete Peeters	Boston Bruins
1982	Billy Smith	New York Islanders
1981	Denis Herron, Michel Larocque, & Richard Sevigny	Montréal Canadiens
1980	Don Edwards & Bob Sauve	Buffalo Sabres
1979	Ken Dryden & Michel Larocque	Montréal Canadiens
1978	Ken Dryden & Michel Larocque	Montréal Canadiens
1977	Ken Dryden & Michel Larocque	Montréal Canadiens
1976	Ken Dryden	Montréal Canadiens
1975	Bernie Parent	Philadelphia Flyers
1974	Tony Esposito	Chicago Blackhawks tied Bernie Parent
1973	Ken Dryden	Montréal Canadiens

Vezina Trophy Winners (continued)

Year	Player	Team
1972	Tony Esposito & Gary Smith	Chicago Blackhawks
1971	Eddie Giacomin & Gilles Villemure	New York Rangers
1970	Tony Esposito	Chicago Blackhawks
1969	Glenn Hall & Jacques Plante	St. Louis Blues
1968	Rogatien Vachon & Gump Worsley	Montréal Canadiens
1967	Glenn Hall & Denis DeJordy	Chicago Blackhawks
1966	Gump Worsley & Charlie Hodge	Montréal Canadiens
1965	Johnny Bower & Terry Sawchuk	Toronto Maple Leafs
1964	Charlie Hodge	Montréal Canadiens
1963	Glenn Hall	Chicago Blackhawks
1962	Jacques Plante	Montréal Canadiens
1961	Johnny Bower	Toronto Maple Leafs
1960	Jacques Plante	Montréal Canadiens
1959	Jacques Plante	Montréal Canadiens
1958	Jacques Plante	Montréal Canadiens
1957	Jacques Plante	Montréal Canadiens
1956	Jacques Plante	Montréal Canadiens
1955	Terry Sawchuk	Toronto Maple Leafs
1954	Harry Lumley	Toronto Maple Leafs
1953	Terry Sawchuk	Detroit Red Wings
1952	Terry Sawchuk	Detroit Red Wings
1951	Al Rollins	Toronto Maple Leafs
1950	Bill Durnan	Montréal Canadiens
1949	Bill Durnan	Montréal Canadiens
1948	Turk Broda	Toronto Maple Leafs
1947	Bill Durnan	Montréal Canadiens
1946	Bill Durnan	Montréal Canadiens
1945	Bill Durnan	Montréal Canadiens
1944	Bill Durnan	Montréal Canadiens
1943	Johnny Mowers	Detroit Red Wings
1942	Frank Brimsek	Boston Bruins
1941	Turk Broda	Toronto Maple Leafs
1940	David Kerr	New York Rangers
1939	Frank Brimsek	Boston Bruins

Vezina Trophy Winners (continued)

Year	Player	Team
1938	Tiny Thompson	Boston Bruins
1937	Normie Smith	Detroit Red Wings
1936	Tiny Thompson	Boston Bruins
1935	Lorne Chabot	Chicago Blackhawks
1934	Chuck Gardiner	Chicago Blackhawks
1933	Tiny Thompson	Boston Bruins
1932	Chuck Gardiner	Chicago Blackhawks
1931	Roy Worters	New York Americans
1930	Tiny Thompson	Boston Bruins
1929	George Hainsworth	Montréal Canadiens
1928	George Hainsworth	Montréal Canadiens
1927	George Hainsworth	Montréal Canadiens

Notes on Sources

Allen, Kevin and Bob Duff. *Without Fear: Hockey's 50 Greatest Goaltenders*. Chicago: Triumph Books, 2002.

Brodeur, Denis and Daniel Daignault. *Goalies: Guardians of the Net*. Montréal: Les Editions de L'Homme, 1995.

Diamond, Dan and Eric Zweig. *Hockey's Glory Days: The 1950s and '60s*. Kansas City: Andrews McMeel Publishing, 2003.

Diamond, Dan, ed. *Total NHL*. Toronto: Dan Diamond and Associates, 2003.

Dryden, Ken. *The Game*. Toronto: Wiley Press, 2005.

Hunter, Douglas. *A Breed Apart*. Toronto: Viking Press, 1995.

Leonetti, Mike. *Canadiens Legends: Montreal's Hockey Heroes*. Vancouver: Raincoast Books, 2003.

McDonnell, Chris. *Hockey's Greatest Stars: Legends and Young Lions*. Willowdale: Firefly Books, 1999.

O'Brien, Andy and Jacques Plante. *The Jacques Plante Story*. Toronto: McGraw-Hill Ltd, 1972.

Podnieks, Andrew, et al. *Kings of the Ice: A History of World Hockey*. Richmond Hill: NDE Publishing, 2002.

Turowetz, Allan and Goyens, Chrys. *Lions In Winter*. Scarborough: Prentice Hall, 1986.

J. Alexander Poulton

J. Alexander Poulton is a writer and photographer and has been a genuine enthusiast of Canada's national pastime ever since seeing his first hockey game. His favourite memory was meeting the legendary gentleman hockey player Jean Beliveau, who in 1988 towered over the young awe-struck author.

He earned his B.A. in English Literature from McGill University and his graduate diploma in Journalism from Concordia University. He has five other books to his credit: *Canadian Hockey Record Breakers, Greatest Moments in Canadian Hockey, Greatest Games of the Stanley Cup, The Montreal Canadians* and *The Toronto Maple Leafs.*